GROUND COVER
PLANTS

GROUND COVER PLANTS

Janet Browne

WARD LOCK LIMITED · LONDON

ACKNOWLEDGEMENTS

The publishers gratefully acknowledge the following agencies for granting permission to reproduce the cover photographs: Harry Smith Horticultural Photographic Collection (pp. 2, 31, 34, 39, 51, 54, 82 and 91); A–Z Collection (p. 42); Michael Warren (pp. 43, 46, and 83); Pat Brindley (cover, pp. 47, 50, 55, 59, 75, 78 and 79). The photograph on p. 67 was taken by Bob Challinor.

All the line drawings are by Nils Solberg.

Front cover: Sedum 'Ruby Glow' *(foreground)* with *Centaurea gymnocarpa* and *Ruta graveolens* courtesy Harry Smith Horticultural Photographic Collection.

First published in Great Britain in 1988
by Ward Lock Limited, 8 Clifford Street
London W1X 1RB, an Egmont Company

House editor Denis Ingram
Text filmset in Bembo
by Hourds Typographica, Stafford, England.

Printed and bound in Portugal by Resopal

British Library Cataloguing in Publication Data
Browne, Janet
    Ground cover plants. – (Concorde
    gardening).
    1. Ground cover plants
    I. Title   II. Series
    635.9'64   SB432

    ISBN 0–7063–6629–8

Frontispiece: Mixed planting with (foreground, left to right) *Vinca major* 'Elegantissima', *Alchemilla mollis* and *Stachys lanata*.

CONTENTS

PREFACE

As gardens become smaller, or large gardens cannot be maintained as they were in the past because of lack of time and labour, so methods of simplifying maintenance are sought because, at the same time, an attractive all-the-year-round place of interest is desired.

To achieve this objective, plants which cover the ground with a dense canopy of leaves and shoots, and thus prevent weed growth, are becoming more and more highly sought after. Fortunately, these ground covering plants also require little care and attention once established and give many years of interest.

There are many plants available which will serve well the purpose of covering the ground. Not all need be prostrate or low growing; some can reach quite a height and become specimen features and thus give variation in the final landscaped effect of the garden.

The major part of this book is devoted to the description of suitable plants for ground cover, be they for temporary use, such as annuals, biennials or bedding out plants, or of a permanent nature, such as herbaceous plants, shrubs, climbers, ramblers, ferns and ornamental grasses. Although requiring attention during the summer months, lawns are also included as they form one of the best ground coverers available for large areas. Throughout, the average height and spread of a plant is given, to enable a selection of suitable plants to be chosen for any type of site. By careful choice, a collection of plants that give interest all the year round can be made.

Chapters are also included on the use, buying, planting, general maintenance and methods of propagation of ground cover plants.

Whatever the size, and wherever the garden, there are ground covering plants which are suitable for growing in a variety of climatic and soil situations, and those discussed in this book offer a wide selection for the discerning gardener, who wishes to enjoy his garden to the full with the minimum of maintenance.

J.B.

CHAPTER 1

WHAT ARE GROUND COVER PLANTS?

Quite literally, ground cover plants are those plants which, with their leaves and stems, cover the ground to give it a decorative appearance, smother weeds, soften hard edges of rock or stone, require minimum maintenance, and generally grow wider in spread than in height. As a bonus, many offer attractive flowers and fruits, or their leaves are of various colours.

Strictly speaking, therefore, a ground cover plant should be one that is evergreen, dense growing and needs little or no attention. In practice, however, this is not always the case; many garden plants make good ground coverers although they are deciduous (lose their leaves in winter), slow to form a carpeting effect, require weeding until established or, like lawns, need regular maintenance at certain times of the year. Nevertheless, such plants require recognition because they can often serve certain purposes where others will not. Equally, some plants, such as climbers and ramblers, which in gardens we consider solely suitable for growing up or over structures or tree trunks, are equally suitable for covering the ground, especially steep banks which would be difficult to mow, or for tumbling down walls. Also, a garden plant that can be termed a ground coverer need not grow merely at soil level – it can be one that grows quite tall but which has an arching, spreading habit and so precludes the growth of other plants, particularly weeds, below it.

With the wide range of plants that can be used, it is, therefore, not a difficult matter to select suitable ones for various positions in the garden, be it large or small. It is also quite possible to create a garden completely with ground cover plants and thus reduce its care and maintenance to the minimum.

In most instances, however, a mixture of plants is required. For example, tall plants are needed to form hedges, screens or focal points, and perhaps a shrub border, rock garden, rose garden or one or more herbaceous or mixed borders are an essential part of the design. In large gardens, wild or woodland areas may be created, and large quantities of plants required as underplants, whereas in a very small town garden there is perhaps only space for a few ground coverers to soften the 'hardness' of patios, containers or paved areas. Whatever the style and layout of the garden, however, there is always room for several or many ground covering plants which will be a pleasure to the eye and labour-saving to maintain. By careful selection from the lists in this book it is possible to choose the right plant for the right position and give it the growing conditions it requires; it will then be not only a good ground coverer but a feature of interest for all, or a greater part, of the year.

To sum up, good cover plants should be:

1 those that cover the ground well and smother weeds, be they perennial evergreens, deciduous plants, shrubs, alpines, herbaceous plants, climbers, ramblers, bedding plants, annuals, ferns, or grasses and their substitutes;
2 hardy whenever possible, though for temporary use bedding plants and annuals serve their purpose until such time as permanent planting can be carried out;
3 of interest, either at certain times of the year when in flower, fruit or with attractive leaves, or be evergreens, with green, variegated or other coloured foliage, which makes them interesting throughout the year;
4 sufficiently vigorous and quick growing to serve the purpose of covering the ground as soon as possible;
5 versatile enough to withstand a variety of average growing conditions, though obviously only certain plants will grow well in very acidic or alkaline soils, or in deep shade or hot sunny positions;
6 those that require as little maintenance as possible.

PRINCIPAL DIVISIONS OF
GROUND COVER GROUPS

Ground cover plants create their ground covering effect by a variety of means and when selecting plants for this purpose it is often helpful to know before setting them out what their ultimate shape will be and how they spread. It is also useful to know the ultimate dimensions of each plant, so average heights and spreads are given of the plants listed in the following chapters. This enables one to decide such points as to how many plants are required, where best to place them in the garden and how to propagate further plants if desired.

CLUMP FORMERS
Mainly herbaceous perennials, annuals and bedding plants which form clumps from a central rootstock.

CARPETERS

Herbaceous plants, shrubs and alpines which form a carpet by means of surface runners or stems, or a prostrate growth habit, which keeps them at, or just above, the soil surface. Many of these root themselves as they grow.

SPREADERS

Mainly herbaceous plants or shrubs which increase their size by underground shoots or roots which grow horizontally and throw up fresh top growth.

HUMMOCKS

Usually shrubs which form a dense rounded bush.

SPRAWLERS

Loose-growing shrubs, climbers and ramblers with floppy stems which drop to ground level as well as producing some erect growths.

CREEPERS

Climbers or ramblers which produce long shoots which spread over the ground, often rooting at intervals.

TWINERS

Plants, usually climbers, which have stems which grow in a spiral manner and, when grown on the flat, will form a tangled mass of growth and, like creepers, can root at intervals.

CHAPTER 2

SELECTING GROUND COVER PLANTS

Before buying any plants for the garden it is always wise to know something about the condition of the soil, the weather conditions in your area, and what grows well and what does not. Much of this information can be found out by seeing what is growing well in neighbouring gardens.

CHECKING SOIL CONDITIONS

If rhododendrons, azaleas and heathers are flourishing, then the soil is almost certainly acid, whereas if plants such as berberis, cotoneaster, hedera, hypericum and vinca are thriving, then it is more likely that the soil is alkaline (chalky). On the other hand, if most plants appear to be growing well, then you may be a lucky gardener who has a more or less neutral soil which, by the addition of peat will give acidic conditions and by applications of chalk will give alkaline ground, thus making it possible to grow a very wide range of plants.

The most certain method of all, however, to find out the pH (acidity or alkalinity) of your soil is by testing it with one of the proprietary soil testing kits available on the market. Take soil samples from various parts of the garden as the pH may vary from different sites. (pH7 is neutral, under is acid and over is alkaline).

Next find out what type of soil you have. When it is not too dry or too wet, take a handful and rub it through your fingers. If it is crumbly and clean it is probably loam – the best of all which only needs regular feeding and humus matter to keep it in good condition. A dust-like soil is a poor starved one, requiring plenty of fertilizers, humus and water. A gritty sample indicates sand and requires the same treatment as starved soil. A spongy black or brown sample indicates an acid peaty soil which will require the addition of lime, unless acid plants, such as rhododendrons, azaleas and most heathers, are to be grown. Soil with white particles in it is chalky and will need peat and fertilizers. A soil that is hard to crumble, and which is sticky when wet and forms clods when dry, indicates clay and will require regular liming and manuring to improve it.

Next find out how moisture-retentive the soil is, so that you know whether it is free draining or not. This information may also be available from neighbours, but if not dig a hole 90 cm (3 ft) deep and 90 cm (3 ft) square and see what happens after heavy rain. No water in the hole after two or three days indicates very free-draining land. No water after seven to ten days means good, average drainage, but water after that length of time indicates poor-draining, moisture-retaining, damp soil.

If the soil is too free draining for your requirements, add annually plenty of humus-forming matter such as compost, peat or shredded bark to help retain moisture. Conversely, these same materials help to improve an over-wet soil by aerating the soil particles. In particularly sodden places, either grow only those plants which will tolerate such conditions, or make one or more soakaways to help drainage. (Soak-aways are made by digging out holes 1 m (3¼ ft) square and deep, filling the lower half with brick and rubble and the top half with soil.)

CHECKING THE GARDEN CLIMATE

Obviously some parts of the country are warmer than others but within each garden there are also climatic variations. Parts may be hot or cold, some areas may be affected by cold draughty winds, there may be low-lying, sheltered areas that attract frost, some spots may get more moisture when it rains than others, some places may be permanently shaded while others get plenty of sun. Investigation and experience will establish these factors, which must be taken into account before planning what ground cover plants to buy and where to site them.

PLANNING BEFORE PLANTING

Whatever the size of your garden, and whether it is virgin land, a well-maintained or neglected one, it is always advisable to plan in advance what ground coverers are going to be best for your purpose.

In a small town or patio garden, there will probably be room for only a few ground cover plants and these should be chosen with care so that they do not become too invasive and remain in proportion with the area available – containers, walls or paving cracks – into which they will be planted. While it is possible in these conditions to have the whole garden planted with ground coverers this could possibly prove dull and flat, and the inclusion of some seasonal flowering plants, specimen subjects and one or two upright growing plants will give an overall effect which is more pleasing to the eye and yet still cover the ground.

Larger gardens offer considerably more scope for planting ground coverers. Not only can they form the groundwork to herbaceous borders, rose beds, shrub borders and rock gardens, but whole areas can be devoted to them in wild or woodland positions and the larger subjects can be grown to advantage to look most attractive, as well as being labour-saving in maintenance.

If the garden is a new one, a proper plan of it, drawn to scale on paper, with existing features marked in, should be prepared and on this the proposed plants, and the areas to be allotted to them, should be indicated. In this way a careful combination of different types of plants can be selected to give a proper landscaped appearance, and you will not be tempted to buy on impulse too many of the wrong types of plants for the wrong places! An existing well-kept or neglected garden should be considered similarly, but never be in a hurry to discard plants or destroy whole areas until you are sure of what you have got, and it may take a full year to find this out.

Finally, before purchasing your ground cover plants, make sure you have selected suitable ones, both to grow in the manner in which you wish them to and those that are suitable for the conditions in your garden. If in any doubt, consult the nurseryman or garden centre from which you propose to purchase the plants.

CHAPTER 3

BUYING AND PLANTING

To achieve the desired results and obtain maximum effect, it is important to buy your plants wisely and plant them correctly in well prepared soil and give them the immediate after-treatment they require in order to become well established.

PURCHASING PLANTS

If obtaining plants from a mail-order nursery, first ensure that it has a good reputation for dispatching healthy, well-grown plants which will arrive in good condition. Then get your order in as soon as possible as most nurserymen deal with orders received on a first-come-first-served basis. Nearly all herbaceous plants, shrubs and trees can be planted between late autumn and late spring when weather and soil conditions are suitable, so expect, and be ready to receive them during that period.

Plants can also be bought from good garden centres and, as most of them will be container grown, i.e. grown in pots, it is quite possible to buy and plant them at any time of year. Always select healthy plants, and make sure that the roots are not growing extensively outside the pot and turned brown. It is also best not to choose plants that are in full flower. Both these points could mean that the plants will make a slow start of fresh growth when planted in your garden.

If purchasing bedding plants, either in pots or boxes, make sure the previous points apply to them also.

PREPARING THE GROUND

Good soil preparation is essential for new plants, especially for those that are to remain in position for a long period. Fork over the ground thoroughly or, if a large area is to be cultivated for ground coverers, hire a mechanical cultivator to save time and effort, and remove all weeds. If the ground is very weedy, it is as well to remove these by an application of a suitable general-purpose non-residual weedkiller before commencing cultivation; this will kill all the weeds and their roots and ensure a clean beginning for the ground coverers, which is essential to give them a quick start into new growth without competition. Suitable weedkillers are those containing glyphosate, paraquat or diquat. Aminotriazole is a total residual weedkiller and the ground must remain unplanted for about three months after its use.

During cultivation work into the lower soil as much organic matter, such as well-rotted compost, peat, pulverized or shredded bark or similar materials as possible. Following this, an application of a general-purpose fertilizer, plus Nitro-chalk if necessary, to the top soil is advisable and this can be hoed or forked in. Then allow the ground to settle naturally for a week or so, or tread it firm with the feet.

PLANTING

Mail-order plants, which may arrive with their roots balled in soil, in pots, or with no root soil, are best planted as soon as possible – weather and soil conditions permitting. If conditions are not suitable, unwrap the plants and either heel them into a trench in a sheltered part of the garden, or store them in a frost-proof place with damp straw or hessian over their roots. Container-grown plants can be left in their containers in a

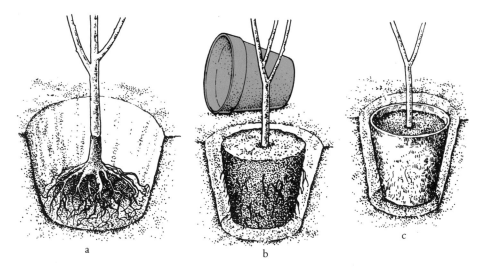

Fig. 1 Various planting methods. (*a*) Bare-root plants – ensure planting hole is sufficiently large to accommodate comfortably the roots and deep enough to ensure that the soil level on stem remains unchanged. (*b*) Container-grown plant – slip or cut off container and plant the complete root ball with as little disturbance as possible. (*c*) A plant in peat pot – the plant can be planted out in the pot as the walls of the pot allow the roots to penetrate through them.

sheltered, frost-free place until conditions improve, provided they are watered during dry periods in summer.

Always make the planting hole large enough to accommodate the plant's roots or container root ball comfortably and ensure that the soil level will finally be the same as that of the plant's previous position, indicated by the soil mark, or marks, on the stem or stems (Fig. 1).

Set each plant in its carefully prepared hole and work soil around the roots carefully with the fingers. In the case of container-grown plants, merely slip or cut the container off and plant the complete root ball with as little disturbance as possible. If the plants are in peat pots, they can be planted out directly in these. Then fill the hole with the remaining soil and firm it in by light treading with the foot. Lightly hoe or rake over the planting areas to leave a tidy appearance.

The distance apart at which the plants are to be set is a matter of choice. They can either be set fairly close together and then thinned later and the unwanted plants put elsewhere in the garden, or they can be planted at the distance to which they will spread at maturity. In the former case a quicker ground covering effect is achieved but work will be necessary on thinning later, and in the second instance, bare soil will show for one or more years. However, bare soil areas can be filled temporarily with annuals, biennials, bedding plants or bulbs to give seasonal colour, provided they do not interfere with the growth of the permanent ground cover plants. On balance, it is generally best to fill the bare soil with ground coverers and concentrate on getting them to grow vigorously by feeding, watering, and weeding when necessary. Bulbs, incidentally, can often be grown among prostrate-type ground coverers, as they push their leaves and flower stems above and give a pretty effect at different seasons of the year.

IMMEDIATE AFTER CARE

After planting, if you are likely to be in doubt about the name of the plants, label them. There is nothing more infuriating than to acquire an unusual plant and then not to be able to remember its name. Next, water in the plants thoroughly to help the soil settle around the roots. Continue to water whenever necessary, particularly container-grown plants which are set out in spring, summer or autumn during dry periods; it also helps to give these an overhead sprinkling to keep the foliage fresh (Fig. 2). Once new growth has commenced, daily attention to watering is less necessary.

It is also advisable to remove flower heads from newly set-out plants to

Fig. 2 Newly set-out plants need frequent and regular watering in spring, summer and autumn. An occasional overhead sprinkling keeps the foliage fresh.

encourage them to put their efforts into fresh root and shoot growth.

If any perennial plants are not fully hardy until established, and have been described as such in the later chapters of this book, give them immediate protection after planting, in the form of cloches, straw held in place by twigs or netting, or hessian screens. Repeat this each winter until the plants are growing strongly. If annual or biennial bedding plants are to be used for summer bedding ground cover, make sure these are not set out until after the last of the late spring frosts.

CHAPTER 4

GENERAL GROUND COVER MAINTENANCE

Although ground covering plants are usually ones requiring minimum maintenance, there are certain jobs that will need attention from time to time if the full benefit and effect required is to be achieved. Certainly, in the first year or two it pays ample dividends to give many of the permanent plants attention so that thereafter they can virtually look after themselves. When in their final positions, bedding plants and annuals, which are only temporary ground coverers, need little attention, other than watering, feeding and dead heading, until it is time to discard them at the end of the season.

FEEDING

However fertile the soil, plants will respond to at least an annual dressing of a general-purpose fertilizer. This is best applied in granular form in the spring and lightly hoed in, if it is possible to get through the leaves and stems. If not, applications of liquid fertilizer in late spring and during the summer will be beneficial. For acid-loving plants it may also be necessary to apply a Sequestrene compound once a year to give the nutrients required, especially on chalky soil.

WEEDING

Until established, it is essential to remove weeds from among young ground coverers whenever they are noticed. If this is not done there is a danger of the weeds smothering the young plants as well as the fact that they compete for food, light and moisture. Hand weeding is without doubt the best method as there is no danger to the ground cover plants. Hoeing can be carried out if great care is taken not to damage the young plant's root system. The application of chemical weedkillers at this stage is not recommended because of the possibility of damaging the cultivated plants.

Sheets of black polythene round the ground coverers until they are growing freely will also smother weeds (Fig. 3). Hold in place with bricks or stones and make sure the cultivated plants receive adequate water.

Fig. 3 To smother weeds which might otherwise compete with newly established ground cover plants, use sheets of black polythene as shown. Note the use of bricks to keep sheet flat.

MULCHING

Mulching serves three purposes; it helps keep the soil in good condition as it gradually gets worked in; it aids the retention of soil moisture; and it helps smother weeds. If 5–8 cm (2–3 in) layers of humus-forming matter such as well-rotted compost (or farmyard manure if available) or products such as pulverized or shredded bark or peat are applied annually each spring when the soil is moist, it will be particularly beneficial. Make sure it is put on the soil between the plants, or under their branches and leaves so these are not smothered by it.

PEST AND DISEASE CONTROL

As with other garden plants, ground coverers can suffer from attacks of pests and diseases. As soon as any symptoms are noticed, prompt remedial action should be taken by applying the correct pesticides. Lack of space precludes making a detailed list of problems and pesticide controls: do seek advice from a reputable source if problems occur.

WATERING

Once ground cover plants are established, and provided they have been mulched, it is rarely necessary to water artificially. However, in their early stages of growth regular watering during dry periods is important to keep the plants growing steadily. How much water and how often it is applied is dependent upon whether the plants like moist or dry soil and this must be gauged by the appearance of the plants. If they look as if they are going to wilt, water them.

TRAINING

To restrain certain plants and to keep them acting as ground coverers, especially climbers and ramblers, it is sometimes necessary to hold low-growing shoots down to soil level to achieve the desired effect. This can be done with bricks or stones, or U-shaped pieces of wire, or wooden pegs (like tent pegs), placed at intervals along the stems. This is especially useful when training plants on steep banks, to get the arrangement you want (Fig. 4).

Fig. 4 To help certain plants act as ground coverers, hold low-growing shoots down to the soil with wooden pegs or U-shaped pieces of wire.

PRUNING

Pruning ground cover plants can usually be kept to the minimum. It may be necessary to trim back the shoots of over-vigorous types, or to cut back those that become straggly to encourage fresh growth, but other than that it usually only involves the removal of dead flower heads where recommended, particularly of annuals and bedding plants, and any dead or unwanted shoots.

Where lawns, or wild areas with grass are involved as ground cover, regular cutting of the former and the occasional topping of the latter (see Chapter 6) will be required between spring and autumn.

THINNING

If ground cover plants such as herbaceous plants and some shrubs get too overgrown, it may become necessary to thin them. This is best done by division of the rootstocks at intervals, when the fresh young outer growths from the clumps can be pulled off and replanted while the central, often dead part, can be discarded.

WINTER PROTECTION

Although almost all plants recommended as ground coverers in this book are fully hardy, occasionally some are rather tender until established. If this is the case, protect them from cold winds or frost in winter with cloches, hessian screens or straw held in place with twigs or netting. Remove the protection as soon as possible in the spring.

CHAPTER 5

INCREASING STOCK

Where large quantities of ground cover plants are required, or where high cost has forced you to buy fewer plants than you really need, it is not a difficult matter to raise new plants yourself from existing stocks. In some instances, buying packets of seeds may be necessary, especially for annuals, biennials and bedding plants generally, but these are not very costly items.

DIVISION

This is the easiest method of increasing plants. There are several ways in which it can be done. The easiest is just to pull off by hand a rooted portion of an established plant, and replant it where you wish. Another method is to use a sharp knife or sharp spade and literally cut out part of an existing clump or carpet so that you have pieces of roots and shoots which can be set out in the required position. The third method, most often used when plants need dividing anyway because the central parts are dying away (this applies particularly to herbaceous perennial clumps), is to lift the plant entirely. Then, using two forks, inserted back to back in the clump, lever it apart and break it up into smaller pieces. Use the fresh outside growths for replanting and discard the worn out inner section. Division is best carried out in autumn or spring.

LAYERING

Many ground coverers will root themselves automatically as their runners or stems grow at soil level. When it is obvious a new plant has been formed, the stem can be severed with a sharp knife on the parent plant side, and the young plant lifted and planted elsewhere. Where a plant cannot, or does not, layer itself easily, it can be helped to do so by nicking the underside of the stem and pegging it down into the soil (which has had some bone meal and humus matter worked into it), with a U-shaped piece of wire, or piece of wood shaped like a tent peg (Fig. 5). Even putting a stone or brick either side of the nicked stem will work well. It may take months, or even a year or two, for new roots and shoots

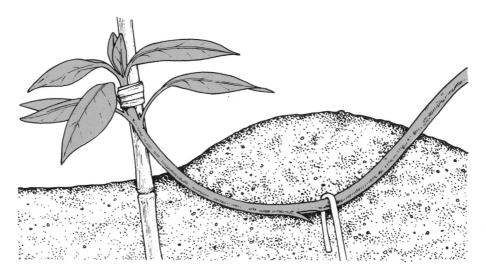

Fig. 5 Encourage the layering of a plant by nicking the underside of a long and low-growing shoot and peg it down into the soil. Tying the tip to a vertical cane will encourage the new plant to grow in an erect manner.

to be formed to make a new plant, but when the youngster is seen to be growing freely it can be severed from its parent, lifted and planted where required.

STEM CUTTINGS

Most shrubs and many herbaceous plants can be increased by cuttings taken of non-flowering side shoots or stems in summer or autumn. It is generally best to use current year's stems and the length will vary according to the size of the plant. Also, some plants root better if a heel – a piece of the old wood – is attached to the base. Remove any lower leaves, trim the base with a sharp knife, and insert the cutting either into the open ground where peat and sand have been mixed with the soil, or in pots or boxes containing a peat, sand and soil mixture, or a proprietary cutting compost, and place these in a frame (Fig. 6). An alternative method is to place each cutting in a peat pot filled with proprietary potting compost. This means that when the new plant is ready to be transplanted to its final position, it can be set out, complete with pot (which will break down in the soil), resulting in the minimum of root disturbance. Water the cuttings as necessary and when fresh growth is well under way the new plants will be ready for planting out, preferably in autumn or spring.

ROOT CUTTINGS

Some herbaceous plants can be propagated by root cuttings. It is not always necessary to lift the plants to obtain these as careful removal of the soil round the plants often reveals strong enough pieces of root for this purpose. Cut them off – pieces about 5 cm (2 in) long – with a slanting cut at the base, and insert them in pots or boxes of sandy compost, either in a cool greenhouse or frame.

Fig. 6 Stem cuttings. (*a*) Taking a cutting from a non-flowering side shoot or stem. (*b*) Cutting with heel (piece of old wood) attached. (*c*) Cuttings inserted in peat/ sand/soil mixture and placed in frame.

SEEDS

Many plants can be raised from seeds. Those of hardy plants, including biennials, can be raised in a special seed bed prepared for them outdoors. Others, such as hardy annuals, can be sown *in situ* (see Chapter 7). Bedding-out plants will require the encouragement of a heated green-house or frame for good germination, and are sown in pots or boxes of a special seed sowing compost in late winter; before planting out harden them off gradually.

CHAPTER 6

GRASSED AREAS

Areas covered with grass offer one of the most effective ground covering methods possible. So often we take lawns and grass paths for granted as part of the garden scene but, if we stop to think about them, they serve a multitude of purposes and, once established, require relatively little maintenance to keep them in good condition and give areas of green that are with us all year and act as foils to the other plants we grow. Areas of rough grass in large gardens, especially when attractively landscaped with shrubs and other plants, are highly effective and very labour-saving also. But grasses are not the only plants which can be used to cover large areas for permanent greenness and these substitutes will also be mentioned in this chapter.

GRASS LAWNS

Starting a new lawn from seed is generally preferable to laying turf as you have the opportunity to decide exactly what type of finish you wish to achieve – a very fine effect or a more hardwearing area for everyday use. In any case, thorough preparation of the soil is necessary with a fine soil tilth and an absence of weeds being essential prior to sowing. The best time to sow a new lawn is in early autumn or spring.

As there are so many excellent grass seed mixtures on the market for all purposes, it is best to purchase one of these rather than to attempt to make up your own mixture. In all cases the sowing rate is 30–50 g per sq m (1–$1\frac{1}{2}$ oz per sq yd).

For a very fine finish which will stand close mowing – 8–11 mm ($\frac{5}{16}$ – $\frac{7}{16}$ in) – select a mixture that contains *Agrostis tenuis*, browntop bent grass, and *Festuca* species, fescues, only. These fine-leaved grasses give neat compact turf and tend to minimize the invasion of weeds. For a slightly more hardwearing mixture, select one containing *Poa trivialis*, in addition to the other two grasses.

Where a hardwearing lawn is required, buy a mixture that contains *Lolium perenne*, perennial ryegrass which, with its broader leaves, will withstand tough usage, but the other grasses mentioned previously, which should also be included, will help keep a close-knit pleasing-looking sward. This type of lawn needs moving less frequently than the finer ones, and should be cut only to a height of about 2.5 cm (1 in).

There are also available special purpose grass seed mixtures for difficult situations, such as dry soils, wet soils, or soils in shade, and these will contain other grasses such as *Phleum bertolonii*, Timothy, *Cynosurus cristatus*, crested dog's tail and *Deschampsia flexuosa*, wavy hair grass. Again, it is best not to mow these grasses lower than 2.5 cm (1 in).

One slight disadvantage of starting new lawns from seed is that care has to be taken during the first season not to over use them. For this reason, also perhaps because an instant finish is required, some people prefer to lay turf. This can be done from autumn to winter or early spring when the weather is suitable. It is important to buy turf from a reputable source to ensure a good mixture of weed-free grasses. Turfing is always more expensive than seeding and, except for small areas, the lower cost of seeding, and generally far better finish, outweigh the slight disadvantage of temporary lack of usage as far as large areas are concerned.

All lawns should be well maintained by feeding, weeding, mowing and edging as necessary, as few things look more unsightly than an ill-kept or neglected lawn.

ROUGH GRASS AREAS

Where areas of grass are to be left rough and mown only once or twice a year – because of the trees, shrubs and bulbs planted in them – one of the cheap hardwearing lawn mixtures will serve the purpose well. In difficult or very dry situations, the addition of *Festuca longifolia* 'Scaldis', the hard fescue, to the mixture will ensure good coverage. If indigenous species of wild flowers are allowed to grow amongst the grasses, they can add an attractive, natural appearance to the area. It is now possible to buy these wild flower and grass seed mixtures already made up; they should be sown and maintained according to the instructions given by the suppliers. Mowing in early summer and mid autumn, to a height of about 8 cm (3 in), will often improve the look of rough grass areas, but if left to their own devices they grow to about 30 cm (12 in).

ALTERNATIVES TO GRASS

In some instances, particularly where there is not much heavy usage but a largish area requires covering with evergreen plants, it can be a feature of interest to use other subjects instead of grass.

One such plant is *Chamaemelum nobile* 'Treneague', (syn. *Anthemis nobilis*) a non-flowering form of chamomile which gives dense cover, has finely divided mid-green leaves and spreads in a carpeting manner. To make a lawn of this, set the plants 15 cm (6 in) apart in spring in an open sunny position. This will grow about 5 cm (2 in) high and each plant can spread up to 45 cm (1½ ft). Propagate by division in spring. Occasional trimming helps to keep a good dense cover.

Another lawn alternative which is not often tried but can look effective is *Trifolium repens*, wild white clover, particularly the Kentish strain. Its typical clover leaves and white flowers all summer can be an attractive feature. Its height and spread are similar to chamomile, and the same care and maintenance is required. Sowing it at the rate of 10 g per sq m (⅓ oz per sq yd) will give good coverage as its creeping stems spread quickly; the best time for sowing is in late spring.

Thymus, thymes, are sometimes used to give a lawn-like effect over large sites, but as they tend to get bare in places they are best used in planting areas among paving or in rock gardens where they get full sun (see Chapter 8).

An unusual feature for sunny or shady positions could be made using *Cotula potentillina* or *C. squalida*, turf-like plants which form dense carpets very rapidly. The former has green fern-like leaves and the latter bronzy green ferny foliage. Both grow about 5 cm (2 in) high and spread 60 cm (2 ft) or more and can become invasive unless kept in the required area. Propagate by division.

Finally, indigenous mosses make a velvety deep green carpet under trees in damp sites.

CHAPTER 7

ANNUALS, BIENNIALS AND BEDDING PLANTS

In a newly planted garden, or where plants have not reached maturity and there are unsightly gaps and weeds, some annuals, biennials and bedding plants are invaluable for giving lovely splashes of colour in spring and summer as well as serving as temporary ground cover.

Annuals, both hardy and half-hardy, are plants which grow from seed, flower, set seeds, and die in one growing season. Biennials are raised from seed one year for flowering the next and usually die and are discarded thereafter. Bedding plants are either half-hardy annuals or biennials which are sown in one place and then planted in their final positions where they are to flower when they have reached the correct stage of growth and at the appropriate time of year. Spring-flowering bedding plants are set out in autumn; summer ones in early summer when the spring plants are past their best.

Before sowing the seeds of hardy annuals *in situ*, or setting out bedding plants, fork over the soil, remove any weeds, tread the ground firm, and rake to give a good surface tilth. Then sow the seeds, according to the instructions on the packets, or set out the plants at the recommended distance apart. Hardy annual seed sites will almost certainly require protection from birds with twigs or netting and the young plants should be thinned as necessary. Hand weeding or careful hoeing will also probably be required initially until the plants are sufficiently established to smother the weeds for you. The raising of half-hardy plants, biennials and bedding plants is described briefly in Chapter 5 and their general care and maintenance in Chapter 4. If you have no facilities for raising bedding plants from seed, see Chapter 3 about buying them.

There are many annuals, biennials and bedding plants suitable for ground cover purposes, but the following are some of the most useful. All, except where specified, will grow in most soils and prefer sunny positions. The spread measurements given indicate the distance apart at which the plants should be when mature – achieved by thinning hardy annuals or when planting out bedding or half-hardy subjects.

Ageratum
Long-lasting, attractive and bushy half-hardy annual with feathery flower heads of blue, pink or white. The heart-shaped leaves are large in

comparison. Excellent for border edging in any sunny position and soil. Most grow 15–20 cm (6–8 in) tall and spread 30 cm (12 in) or more. Of the blue flowered ageratum, the F_1 hybrids 'Adriatic', 'Blue Mink' and 'Blue Danube' are excellent and contrast well with pink 'Bengali' and white 'Summer Snow', also both F_1 hybrids. Buy as bedding plants or raise from seed sown in heat in early spring.

Alyssum
The annual varieties of *Alyssum maritimum* (syn. *Lobularia maritima*) are easily grown from seed sown *in situ* in late spring or, for earlier flowering, in heat in early spring. The plants form compact clumps or have a creeping habit and are ideal for the front of borders, in rock gardens, on walls, among paving stones or in outdoor containers. Their height is about 10 cm (4 in) or less but spread can be 30 cm (1 ft) or more. Good varieties which produce masses of small flowers for a long period include 'Carpet of Snow' and 'Snow Carpet', white; 'Royal Carpet', deep purple; 'Wonderland', deep red; and 'Rosie O'Day', pink. (See Chapter 8 for perennial varieties.)

Antirrhinum (snapdragon)
Although antirrhinums can be short-lived perennials in warm, sheltered districts, they are best treated as half-hardy annuals for summer bedding out, when they will flower throughout the summer until autumn frosts. The fragrant tubular flowers with upper and lower lips are borne prolifically on six or more spikes and their glowing colours – all except blue – enhance any summer flower or shrub border. There is a vast range of hybrids and varieties from which to choose, from the taller forms up to 90 cm (3 ft) which spread about 45 cm (1½ ft), through intermediate strains and down to the 'Tom Thumb', 'Royal Carpet', 'Magic Carpet' and 'Little Gem' mixtures growing 10–20 cm (4–8 in) high but spreading up to 23 cm (9 in); these latter are excellent for carpeting, rockeries, containers and as edging plants. Raise from seed sown in heat in late winter.

Cheiranthus (wallflower)
Superb biennials for spring flowering, especially when planted with myosotis (forget-me-not, q.v.), to form a colourful carpet as the groundwork for spring bedding schemes. If the plants have the central growing point pinched out when in the early stages of growth, it will encourage bushiness and increase ground coverage and flowering. There are two types of wallflowers – the true ones with glowing velvety flowers of all shades of red, orange, yellow and white (*Cheiranthus cheiri* and its many varieties) and *C. allionii,* the Siberian wallflower, which lasts longer in

flower and is orange or yellow. Both forms have a lovely fragrance. Height is about 23 cm (9 in) for the dwarf types to 60 cm (2 ft) for taller ones and spread 30 cm (1 ft) to 45 cm (1½ ft). Wallflowers are easily raised in an outdoor seed bed in early summer, transplanted 15 cm (6 in) apart when large enough, and planted in their flowering positions in late autumn. They do, however, like a chalky soil, so if the ground is at all acid apply some lime before planting out. Botanically wallflowers are perennials, and will last for several seasons, but they tend to become leggy and are best discarded after the first flowering.

Echium (viper's bugloss)
Two useful forms of the hardy annual *Echium plantagineum* are 'Blue Bedder', and 'Dwarf Hybrids' with a mixture of pink, white, rose, red, blue, purple and mauve bell-shaped flowers borne in profusion. Height and spread are about 30 cm (1 ft). Raise from seed in their flowering position in spring.

Fig. 7 *Eschscholzia* (Californian poppy). A hardy annual with poppy-like flowers in shades of white, yellow, pink, orange and red.

Eschscholzia (Californian poppy) (Fig. 7)
These hardy annuals with single or double poppy-like flowers in shades of white, yellow, pink, orange and red are cheerful plants for filling gaps

as they can be sown where they are to flower in spring. 'Ballerina' and 'Harlequin Hybrids' are good forms to grow for general purposes, reaching a height and spread of about 30 cm (1 ft), while 'Miniature Primrose' and *Eschscholzia caespitosa* 'Sundew', both yellow, make a pretty show as border edging or in the rock garden, growing to a height and spread of about 13 cm (5 in).

Iberis (candytuft)
The hardy annual forms are useful for filling gaps temporarily as they grow fast and produce bushy plants with many dense heads of flowers. Good forms to grow for carpeting purposes are 'Fairy Mixture', 'White', and 'Delicate Pink'; the height of these is about 15 cm (6 in) and the spread some 23 cm (9 in). Easily raised from seed sown *in situ* in spring. (See also *Iberis,* Chapter 8.)

Lathyrus (sweet pea)
Sweet peas are highly popular hardy annuals which are usually treated as climbers by growing them up canes or pea sticks. These tall forms can also be allowed to grow as they wish without support, but the result is generally a somewhat messy tangle of growth with flowers borne on short bent stems. Far more useful as effective and colourful ground cover plants not requiring supports are the dwarf forms which produce really bushy plants with a height of 15 cm (6 in) to 90 cm (3 ft) and a spread of about 90 cm (3 ft). Good varieties in a lovely range of colours include 'Supersnoop', 'Cupid', 'Patio', 'Jet-Set Mixed', and 'Knee Hi Mixed'. Their long season of flowering makes them ideal as low-growing summer hedges, container plants, or border fillers. Seed can be sown *in situ* in spring, or in heat earlier in the year. Sweet peas do best in a rich, well-drained soil. (See also *Lathyrus,* Chapter 10.)

Limnanthes (poached egg flower)
The species most often offered in catalogues is *Limnanthes douglasii,* which is a very easily grown hardy summer annual from seed sown *in situ* in spring for flowering throughout the summer. Given the opportunity, limnanthes will seed itself freely. The flowers are white with a yellow-orange centre and have a slight fragrance. Height and spread are about 15 cm (6 in).

Lobelia
Best grown as half-hardy annuals from seed sown in heat in early spring, two forms of lobelia are useful bedding plants to combat weed invasion. There are the small bushy varieties with a height of 10 cm (4 in) and a spread of 15 cm (6 in), and these include favourites such as 'Cambridge Blue'; 'Crystal Palace', dark blue with bronze leaves; 'Rosamund', crim-

Mysotis alpestris (forget-me-not) is a delightful spring-flowering biennial for ground cover.

son with a white centre; 'White Lady'; 'Mrs Clibran Improved', deep blue with a white eye and 'String of Pearls', mixed colours. Other useful lobelias are the trailing forms, especially good for containers as well as the front of borders, which have a height similar to the bush forms but produce trailing shoots of flowers 30 cm (1 ft) or more long. Good varieties are 'Red Cascade', red, white-eyed flowers; 'Sapphire', deep blue, white eyed; 'Blue Basket', violet-blue; 'Blue Cascade', light blue; and 'Cascade Mixed'. All lobelias have a long season of flowering, from early summer to the first frosts.

Mesembryanthemum (Livingstone daisy)
Delightful annuals of low height 8–10 cm (3–4 in) with a trailing habit that gives them a spread of about 30 cm (1 ft). Their daisy-like flowers, of red, orange, white, yellow or bicolours, are produced in profusion all summer if the plants are in a light soil which gets plenty of sun. These are complemented by succulent leaves which glisten with a silvery coating giving an exotic appearance to the plants. The most usually grown forms are *Mesembryanthemum* (syn. *Dorotheanthus*) *criniflorum* and 'Magic Carpet Mixed', both mixed colours, and 'Lunette', which has yellow petals with a rust-red centre. All three are excellent for border edging, trailing over walls or banks, and creeping among the stones of a rock garden. They are raised by sowing seed in heat in early spring or from an outdoor sowing *in situ* in late spring.

Myosotis (forget-me-not)

This hardy biennial is an ideal carpeter, like cheiranthus (wallflowers), for spring bedding schemes, growing 13–30 cm (5–12 in) high and spreading 15 cm (6 in) or more. The small blue or pink flowers make a colourful sight set against hairy pale green leaves and, if allowed to, the plants will seed themselves freely. They will grow anywhere, except in dense shade, and so have additional uses in the rockery, among paving stones and in flower and shrub borders. There are a number of varieties worth growing, among them 'Royal Blue', 'Ultramarine', 'Miniature Blue', 'Rose Pink', 'White Ball', and 'Carmine King'. Raise from seed sown in a seed bed in early summer, thin seedlings and plant out in summer where they are to flower next spring.

Nemophila (baby blue eyes)

An easily grown hardy annual from seed sown *in situ* in spring, nemophila makes an attractive summer-flowering carpeting plant which keeps weeds at bay. The species usually offered is *Nemophila menziesii* (syn. *N. insignis*) with white-centred blue buttercup-like flowers and pale deeply toothed leaves. Its height and spread is about 23 cm (9 in) and it has the advantage over many annuals in that it performs well in moist and cool situations.

Reseda (mignonette)

This sweetly scented old-fashioned cottage garden hardy annual is returning to popularity and makes a foil for many other summer-flowering plants, with its heads of buff or red coloured blooms and lance-shaped leaves. Catalogues offer forms of *Reseda odorata* such as 'Sweet Scented', buff; 'Machet', red; and 'Crimson Fragrance', and these have a height of about 30 cm (1 ft) and spread about 23 cm (9 in). Raise from seed sown in heat in late winter or *in situ* mid-spring.

Sanvitalia (creeping zinnia)

One of the finest ground covering annuals for edging borders or growing in the rockery is *Sanvitalia procumbens*. It can be sown *in situ* in spring and will form attractive mounds with its trailing stems and produce yellow daisy-like flowers with a black centre for a long period. It grows best in a well-drained soil in a sunny position and reaches a height of about 15 cm (6 in) and spreads 23–30 cm (9–12 in).

Tagetes (African, French and Afro-French marigolds)

No garden of summer flowers is complete without some of the excellent new strains of marigolds. Not only do these half-hardy annuals give a wonderful show of bloom from summer to the first frosts but the shorter forms, in particular, are good ground cover plants. Their flowers, either single and daisy-like, or double and carnation-like, are usually yellow, orange, red or bicoloured and smother the deeply-cut leaves. All are best raised from seed sown in heat in early spring and planted out in early summer. There are many varieties and hybrids from which to choose, but for restricting weed growth select those with a height and spread of around 30–45 cm (1–1$\frac{1}{2}$ ft). The F$_1$ hybrids are more expensive to purchase but they are often worth the extra cost because of their high quality performance. Of African marigolds a good selection would include 'First Lady', 'Gay Ladies', 'Sunshot', 'Moonshot', 'Yellow Galore', 'Gold Galore' and the 'Inca' hybrids. The 'Giant Crested' French marigolds are particularly recommended for covering ground, especially 'Honeycomb', 'Queen Bee', 'Goldfinch' and 'Royal Crested Mixture'; other good French marigolds include the doubles 'Orange Boy' and 'Yellow Boy', and singles 'Silvia', 'Naughty Marietta' and 'Honey'. Among Afro-French hybrids (which do not form seed, have red stems and tend to be more floriferous than most marigolds) are 'Caribbean Parade', 'Showboat', 'Red Seven Star', 'Sunrise' and 'Super Star Orange'.

Tropaeolum (nasturtium)
One of the easiest and most rewarding of hardy annuals is the nasturtium. The large seeds are easily sown *in situ* in late spring and the yellow, orange, red, pink or creamy white trumpet flowers and heart-shaped leaves are borne on trailing stems from early summer until first frosts. They will grow in the poorest of soils but flower best in a sunny postion. Most of those listed in catalogues grow 15–30 cm (6–12 in) in height, but spread 45 cm (1$\frac{1}{2}$ ft) or more. Some good forms from which to choose are the 'Mixed Double Gleam Hybrids', 'Tom Thumb Mixed', 'Jewel Mixed', 'Whirlybird Mixed', 'Empress of India' and 'Alaska' (with green and cream striped leaves). For rough ground or to cover a dry bank or unwanted eyesore, 'Mixed Tall Single' is a semi-climbing strain which will grow about 1.8 m (6 ft) long and make an attractive colourful ground cover plant.

Verbena (vervain)
Growing only 15–30 cm (6–12 in) high but with a trailing habit, verbenas, which are best grown as half-hardy annuals, make useful edging, rockery and carpeting summer blooming plants. Their prolifically flowering stems cover 30 cm (1 ft) or more of ground. Good varieties include 'Giant Mixed'; 'Madame du Barry', carmine-red; 'Rainbow Mixture'; 'Springtime', mixed colours; 'Sparkle', scarlet; 'Showtime' and 'Amethyst', violet-blue. Raise from seed sown in heat in early spring.

Tagetes 'Gold Galore' (African marigold) makes a splendid summer display.

CHAPTER 8

HERBACEOUS PLANTS

Many herbaceous plants make excellent ground cover subjects to suppress and prevent weed growth. Not only are there low-growing types which spread along the ground and grow only a few inches high but there are also taller types which by their spreading habit, bushiness or large leaves prevent weed invasion as well as forming structure or specimen plants in their own right.

As herbaceous plants, also called hardy perennials or herbaceous perennials, usually live for a number of years, consideration must be given before selection and planting as to what their ultimate role in the garden is to be. Large gardens, with space for herbaceous or mixed herbaceous and shrub borders, as well as a rockery and perhaps naturalized or light woodland and boggy areas, obviously can accommodate a large range of these valuable plants. In a small garden, or maybe just a patio area, choice will be restricted and care should be taken to select the right plants for the right purpose in the right place. One or two specimen plants, in containers if necessary, plus a few clump-forming or not too invasive low-growing types, may be all that are necessary to give the desired decorative effect in a labour-saving manner.

Some of the herbaceous plants listed have stems and leaves which die down each winter, but the following spring new top growth appears from the rootstocks. During the period when these deciduous plants are dormant, weeds are unlikely to be a problem, and a peat or shredded bark mulch should take care of the few that might appear before the herbaceous plants start into fresh spring growth. Wherever possible though, it is good sense to make as much use as possible of evergreen plants which are hardy, frost-proof and give colour all the year round. For this reason, many of the following plants recommended are evergreen species or varieties.

As herbaceous plants for ground cover purposes are usually to be employed for their life span it is important to know by what method of growth they suppress weeds. Most come into the categories of clump formers, carpeters or spreaders (see definitions on pp. 8–9) and these are indicated in the following descriptive plant lists. Buying, planting, and care of herbaceous plants are given in Chapters 3 and 4, and the best methods of increasing or renewing stock are covered in Chapter 5, though the method of propagation is mentioned here.

The spread measurements given are also the distances apart at which the plants should be set out. These can only be considered average measurements as plants will vary in their ultimate heights and spreads according to their growing conditions. Except where stated, all the following plants are fully hardy.

Acaena (New Zealand burr)

Carpeter. Evergreen. These New Zealand plants are ideal among paving stones or as a carpet among other subjects as they rapidly form dense mats of growth. The species and variety recommended grow only 5 cm (2 in) high but spread about 60 cm (2 ft). In all cases the summer flowers are insignificant but the autumn burrs are attractive in shades of greens, browns, russet and crimson. Recommended are *Acaena buchananii, A. microphylla* (purple-bronze), *A. pulchella* (bronzy foliage) and 'Copper Carpet'. They prefer a good loamy soil and full sun, but will tolerate light shade. Propagate by division between autumn and spring.

Achillea (yarrow, milfoil)

Mainly carpeters. Most are evergreen. Two good summer-flowering forms for borders are *Achillea millefolium* 'Cerise Queen' (spreader, deciduous), with beautifully coloured flat flower heads and serrated leaves, and 'Moonshine', light yellow flowers and all-the-year-round silvery filigree leaves. They grow to a height of up to 75 cm (2½ ft) and spread about 45 cm (1½ ft). Two good forms from a number for the front of the border or in a rock garden are *Achillea* × 'King Edward', which forms a carpet of greyish leaves with summer flowers of primrose yellow, height 10 cm (4 in), spread 20 cm (8 in); and *A. tomentosa* making a carpet of grey-green leaves with deep yellow summer flowers: height 15 cm (6in) and spread 30 cm (1ft). All achilleas like a well-drained soil and sun. Propagate by root division in spring.

Ajuga (bugle)

Carpeter. Evergreen. Excellent low-growing plants which form good all-the-year-round weed smothering carpets provided they have the moist soil they like; they tolerate both sun and light shade. In adverse growing conditions, the carpets tend to get bare in the centre. Their height is from 10–30 cm (4–12 in) and spread between 45 and 60 cm (1½ and 2 ft). There are a number of good early-summer-flowering species and varieties from which to choose: *A. reptans* 'Braunherz', purple-bronze leaves and deep blue flowers; *A. metallica*, crinkled bronze foliage and deep blue flowers; *A. reptans* 'Burgundy Glow', variegated purple-red leaves, blue flowers; 'Multicolor' (syn.'Rainbow'), bronze, pink and yellow variegated leaves, blue flower spikes, which grows best in sunny position; and 'Variegata', grey-green, cream variegated leaves, blue flowers. Propagate by division at any time.

Alchemilla (lady's mantle)
Clump former. Deciduous. Excellent for producing a dense cover of leaves during the summer, it grows well in most soils, in sun or light shade. *Alchemilla mollis* is most commonly grown and has large round velvety leaves with masses of sprays of tiny yellowish flowers in summer. Height up to 45 cm (1½ ft) and spread about 60 cm (2 ft). *A. alpina* (sometimes sold as *A. conjuncta*) is an attractive low grower for front of borders or rock gardens. The dense mass of silvery green leaves is covered with sprays of small greenish flowers in summer. Its height is about 15 cm (6 in) and spread up to 60 cm (2 ft). Alchemillas seed themselves freely, or may be propagated by division between autumn and spring.

Anthemis (chamomile) (See Chapter 6)

Alyssum
Carpeter. Evergreen. One of the easiest ground cover plants to grow, it is attractive all year with its silvery green stems and leaves. It is ideal for rockeries, in paving gaps, on slopes, over walls, or for carpeting beds of shrubs or roses. It grows best in dry, sunny positions and to prevent the carpet thinning out, trim with shears after its masses of yellow spring flowers are over. *Alyssum saxatile* and its varieties – such as 'Dudley Neville', 'Flore Plenum' and 'Gold Dust' – grow 15–25 cm (6–10 in) tall and spread 45 cm (1½ ft) or more. Propagate by spring-sown seed, layering or cuttings in summer. (See Chapter 7 for annual varieties.)

Anaphalis (pearl everlasting)
Clump former. Deciduous. Only one species – *Anaphalis triplinervis* – is really suitable among this group as a ground cover plant, but its silver-grey mat-forming leaves and white summer 'everlasting' flowers make it an attractive foil for other plants. It grows best in a sunny position and well-drained soil and reaches a height of 30 cm (12 in) with a spread of about 40 cm (16 in). Propagate by division between autumn and spring.

Arabis (rock cress)
Carpeter. Evergreen. Quick-growing and will thrive well anywhere except in wet soils or shady positions; in such places it gets straggly and dies back at the centre. It is excellent for rock gardens, among paving, on walls and for the front of borders. It flowers in late spring or early summer and, like alyssum, is best clipped with shears after flowering.

Varieties of *Arabis albida* (syn. *A. caucasica*) are most commonly grown, and include 'Flore Pleno', greyish green leaves, double white flowers; 'Variegata', cream edged leaves, pink flowers; and 'Rosabella', light green leaves, pink flowers. All grow about 15 cm (6 in) high and spread up to 45 cm ($1\frac{1}{2}$ ft). They seed themselves freely, or can be propagated by division in autumn.

Fig. 8 *Armeria maritima* (thrift). A hardy evergreen perennial, suitable for rock gardens and front of borders. Height about 15 cm (6 in); spread 45 cm ($1\frac{1}{2}$ ft).

Armeria (thrift) (Fig. 8)
Carpeter. Evergreen. Lovely plants for rock gardens, among paving or in the front of borders. They do best in a well-drained soil in full sun. Recommended ones to grow are varieties of *Armeria maritima*, which have dark green, small grass-like leaves and white or pink summer flowers. Good examples are 'Alba', 'Düsseldorf Pride', 'Ruby Glow' and 'Vindictive'. All grow about 15 cm (6 in) high and spread 45 cm ($1\frac{1}{2}$ ft) or more. Propagate by basal summer cuttings, spring division or seed sown in spring.

Artemisia
Sprawling plants, some almost shrubby. Evergreen. For those who like

Alchemilla mollis (lady's mantle) provides dense leaf cover in summer.

Aubrieta 'Dr Mules' is particularly attractive grown in the rockery.

to use aromatic grey-leaved plants as a foil to other green or variegated ones, artemisias are particularly useful. To keep them compact and good weed suppressors, it is advisable to remove their insignificant flowers and trim them back with shears every spring. Among popular varieties are *Artemisia* 'Powys Castle', with its mass of silver filigree foliage growing about 60 cm (2 ft) high with a spread of about 90 cm (3 ft), and 'Silver Queen', which grows similarly and thrives in hot spots. *A. schmidtiana* has lovely lacy foliage (and grey flowers) and grows about 23 cm (9 in) by 45 cm (1½ ft), while its dwarf form *A. s.* 'Nana' is only 8 cm (3 in) high but with a spread of 30–45 cm (1–1½ ft). All like full sun and well drained soil, and grow well in coastal areas. Propagate by division between autumn and spring. (Other popular artemisias tend not to make satisfactory ground cover plants.)

Asarum

Carpeter. Evergreen. *Asarum europaeum* is an ideal ground coverer for cool shady places in rockeries or woodland. Its rounded, leathery, shiny dark green leaves form a dense carpet about 15 cm (6 in) high and 45 cm (18 in) in spread. In spring, insignificant purple-brown bell-shaped flowers are produced. Propagate by division in spring.

Aster (Michaelmas daisy)

Clump former. Deciduous. Although a number of asters make reasonably good ground coverers in herbaceous or mixed borders, especially some of the varieties of *Aster novi-belgii* and *A. novae-angliae*, they tend to require regular division to prevent the centres dying out and the plant performing poorly. However, a useful form for the front of borders or rock gardens is *A. tongolensis* (syn. *A. yunnanensis*), variety 'Berggarten', which produces blue-mauve, orange-centred flowers in early summer; it is almost evergreen. It grows well in a sunny fertile soil and is about 40 cm (16 in) tall by a spread of 30 cm (12 in). Propagate by division between autumn and spring.

Astilbe (syn. *Spiraea*)

Clump former. Deciduous. Easily grown perennials for moist, rich soil in sun or light shade. Their dense deeply toothed foliage (often copper coloured) makes good spring to autumn ground cover and their feathery plumes of minute flowers in a wide range of colours give an exotic appearance in summer. Some of the most dramatic astilbes to grow are the hybrids of *Astilbe × arendsii* which have a foliage height and spread of about 60 cm (2 ft) by 90 cm (3 ft) and flower plumes up to 90 cm (3 ft) tall. Examples of these are 'Amethyst', lilac-rose; 'Bressingham Beauty', pink; 'Deutschland', white; 'Fanal', deep red; 'Federsee', rose red; 'Fire', deep salmon; 'Ostrich Plume', arching and deep pink; and 'Irrlicht', white with dark leaves. For small gardens the smaller forms may be more appropriate, such as *A. simplicifolia* 'Sprite', shell-pink, and *A. chinensis* 'Pumila', lilac-rose; these are about 30 cm (1 ft) in height and spread, with flower plumes 30–45 cm (1–1½ ft) tall. An exquisite miniature is *A. simplicifolia* 'Nana', with arching pink blooms and shiny pale leaves; its height is about 10 cm (4 in) and spread about 20 cm (8 in), with the plumes some 8 cm (3 in) taller. Propagate by division in spring.

Aubrieta

Carpeter. Evergreen. *Aubrieta deltoidea* varieties are most usually grown and all are excellent for edging borders, planting beneath shrubs and roses, and using in the rockery, among paving, on banks and walls. They form carpets of small, grey-green leaves and in spring are covered with heads of pink, purple or blue flowers. The plants grow about 15 cm (6 in) high and spread up to 60 cm (2 ft). Some good varieties are 'Bressingham Red', carmine; 'Dr Mules', violet-purple; 'Maurice Prichard', light pink; 'Red Carpet', deep red; 'Triumphant', blue; and 'Variegata', blue with gold-edged leaves. All like a well drained, preferably limy soil, and plenty of sun. To keep the plants compact and to prevent dead centres, clip them with shears after flowering. Propagate by summer cuttings or division in autumn for the varieties named. Other varieties are listed in seed catalogues for raising from seed, but the resultant plants are regrettably inferior in performance and do not make such good weed smotherers.

Bergenia (syn. *Megasea*)

Clump former. Evergreen. By choosing the evergreen species and hybrids, i.e. not *Bergenia ciliata* or 'Ballawley' which can lose their leaves in a severe winter, these plants are among the best of ground coverers. They will thrive almost anywhere except in very damp soil or deep shade. They have large dark green leaves, which often take on a red tinge or turn maroon in winter, and throw up heads of flowers in spring which are about 30 cm (1 ft) high. The foliage height of the plants varies between 15 and 30 cm (6 and 12 in) and the spread is between 30 and 60 cm (1 and 2 ft). A useful species is *B. cordifolia*, with its heart-shaped leaves and purple-pink flowers. Good hybrids include 'Bressingham Salmon'; 'Bressingham White'; 'Evening Glow' (syn. 'Abendglut'), pinky purple; 'Schmidtii', light pink; 'Silver Light' (syn. 'Silberlicht') and 'Sunningdale', deep pink flowers with deep red-brown leaves in winter. Propagate by root division in autumn or spring.

Brunnera (perennial forget-me-nots)

Clump formers. Deciduous. Although brunneras do not retain their large heart-shaped leaves during the winter, nevertheless they make good ground cover plants for moist, shady positions, especially under trees, though they will grow equally well in moist spots. *Brunnera macrophylla* produces bright sky-blue forget-me-not-like flowers in early summer, while *B.m.* 'Variegata' has less significant flowers but green and cream leaves which develop best in shade. Height and spread for both is about 45 cm (1½ ft). They are best propagated by division in autumn or spring.

Campanula (bell flower)

Clump formers or spreaders. Deciduous or evergreen. This is a genus of many varied and useful garden plants but only some are suitable for ground cover purposes. They grow well in any soil, preferably with some lime in it, and are happy in full sun or light shade; those listed are ideal for borders or rockeries and usually flower for a long period during the summer. For borders, the clump former *Campanula alliariifolia* 'Ivory Bells', (deciduous), with hairy grey-green leaves and 60 cm (2 ft) spikes of bell-shaped white flowers and which grows 30 cm (1 ft) high and spreads 45 cm (1½ ft), is particularly effective, as is also *C. latiloba* 'Percy Piper' (evergreen), a hybrid with similar foliage height and spread and 90 cm (3 ft) spikes of deep blue flowers. For the rock garden or among paving there are a number of forms of *C. carpatica* which are suitable, such as 'Blue Moonlight', light blue; 'Bressingham White'; 'Chewton

Joy', mid-blue; 'Hannah', white; and 'Isobel', deep blue. All are deciduous clump formers growing about 23 cm (9 in) high by 30 cm (1 ft) in spread and they have dense masses of small green leaves. Two other useful alpines with long flowering periods are the spreaders C. *portenschlagiana* (syn. *C. muralis*) (deciduous) and C. *poscharskyana* (evergreen). The former produces a dense mass of small-toothed leaves, spikes of purple-blue flowers, and has a height of about 15 cm (6 in) and spread of 60 cm (2 ft). The latter has more rounded leaves and lavender-blue star flowers, and its height is 30 cm (1 ft) with a spread up to 90 cm (3 ft). Both these species are long lived and tend to become invasive unless cut back from time to time. Propagate all the campanulas mentioned by division in autumn or spring or by spring basal cuttings.

Campanula portenschlagiana (syn. *C. muralis*) (bellflower) is a useful and colourful spreading alpine.

Cerastium (snow in summer) pictured here in winter forming a weed-free ground cover.

Cerastium (snow in summer)

Spreader. Evergreen. *Cerastium tomentosum* is most commonly grown and to prevent it becoming straggly it is best planted in well-drained soil in full sun. It forms dense mats of silvery grey leaves, with a height and spread of about 23 cm (9 in) by 60 cm (2 ft) and produces white star-like flowers in early summer. This species can become invasive when established and it is advisable not to grow it in any position where it could smother any small plants. A less rampant species is *C. tomentosum columnae*, not always easily obtainable, but it forms silvery white 'mats' with white flowers and is generally a neater, smaller plant, but still invasive. Propagate by division in spring.

Dianthus (garden pinks)
Mainly carpeters. Evergreen. These are attractive grey-green grass-like leaved and fragrant single- or double-flowered plants that are ideal for rockeries, walls, border edging, containers and between paving stones. (They should not be confused with carnations, which are usually taller growing and not carpeting plants.) Pinks like a well drained soil, preferably a slightly limy one, and full sun to give of their best. A species commonly grown is *Dianthus deltoides*, which is about 8 cm (3 in) high, spreads about 30 cm (1 ft) and produces masses of pink summer flowers on 23 cm (9 in) stems; its red and white flowering form, *D. d.* 'Brighteyes' and salmon-red flowered *D. d.* 'Flashing Light', are also popular. Two other old-fashioned pinks which have made a come-back in recent years are 'Charles Musgrave', white with a green eye, and 'Mrs Sinkins', white, both growing 23 cm (9 in) by 30 cm (1 ft). Most of the modern pinks are hybrids which flower in early summer and again in early autumn. Those suitable for borders – growing 30–38 cm (12–15 in) in height and spread – include 'Doris', salmon-pink with a deeper centre; 'Constance Finnis', deep pink and white; 'Haytor', white; and 'White Ladies'. Compact dwarf hybrids, again with two seasons of flowering but which only grow to a height of 8–15cm (3–6 in) and spread 15–23 cm (6–9 in), include among the many available 'Little Jock', rose pink; 'Oakington Hybrid', deep rose; 'Garland', pure pink and 'Nyewoods Cream', grey-green leaves and cream flowers. All garden pinks tend to become straggly within three to five years and are generally best replaced by new plants which can easily be raised from summer side-shoot cuttings, division in spring, layers in summer or spring-sown seed.

Dryas
Carpeter. Evergreen. *Dryas octopetala* is an attractive slow-growing but dense mat-forming plant which is ideal for rockeries and among paving. It grows only 5–8 cm (2–3 in) high but will spread 60 cm (2 ft) or more. It has lobed leaves and pretty white early summer flowers followed by fluffy seed heads. It can be planted in any free-draining soil in a sunny position. Propagate by summer heel cuttings or division in spring.

Epimedium (barrenwort, bishop's hat)
Carpeter. Evergreen or deciduous. Very easily grown plants in most types of soil and situations and particularly useful under trees casting light shade. All grow up to about 30 cm (1 ft) high and spread 30 cm (1 ft) also. Not only are their leaves attractive, either green or varigated, but also their dainty spring flowers in a mixture of pale shades. Of the evergreens, *Epimedium perralderianum* 'Frohnleiten', with golden yellow flowers, and 'Sulphureum', pale yellow blooms and leaves with autumn and spring

tints, are particularly useful. Among the deciduous forms, *E. alpinum*, reddish flowers and foliage sometimes flecked brown and red; *E. cantabrigensis*, orange-brown; *E. macranthum* (syn. *E. grandiflorum*), pale pink; and *E. rubrum*, red, are all worthy of a place in the garden. Propagate by division between autumn and spring.

Euphorbia (spurge)

Clump former or spreader. Deciduous or evergreen. Spurges are long-living useful plants which are easy to grow in any reasonably good soil in sun or light shade. Of the evergreen forms, *Euphorbia robbiae*, with rosettes of dark green leaves and tall heads of greenish late spring flowers, is most commonly known and grows about 45 cm (1½ ft) high and spreads 60 cm (2 ft); *E. wulfenii* is similar but a larger plant, reaching a height and spread of up to 1.2 m (4 ft). Both are useful 'fillers' for the border or in shady positions. Among the deciduous types, three good ones to select are *E. griffithii* 'Fireglow', with outstanding early summer orange-red leaf bracts and rich green leaves, 90 cm (3 ft) tall and wide; *E. polychroma* (syn. *E. epithymoides*), sulphur-yellow spring flowers and purple-green leaves, 45 cm (1½ ft) by 60 cm (2 ft); and *E. myrsinites*, an unusual blue-grey leaved plant with trailing stems and early summer yellow flower heads, 15 cm (6 in) by 45 cm (1½ ft). Propagate all by division from autumn to spring.

Geranium (crane's bill)

Clump former or spreader. Deciduous. True geraniums (not to be confused with pelargoniums which are often called geraniums) are very versatile, hardy herbaceous plants and serve many purposes in the garden. They grow well in most soils and positions, in sun or light shade, and withstand drought well. There are many which are ideal ground cover plants, being attractive in both leaf and flower. In most cases the leaves are deeply toothed in varying shades of green and the flowers, usually single but sometimes double, appear in late spring and summer. There are great numbers of geraniums suitable for ground cover use and the following are just a few worth considering. *Geranium endressii* 'A. T. Johnson', silvery pink, and *G. e.* 'Wargrave Pink', clear pink, grow to a height of 40–50 cm (16–20 in) and spread up to 90 cm (3 ft). With these two the old leaves can be left on in winter and will continue to form a cover. *G. macrorrhizum* 'Ingwersen's Variety' is semi-evergreen with foliage which produces good autumn tints after the soft pink flowers. Its height and spread are about 45 cm (1½ ft) by 60 cm (2 ft). Another semi-evergreen geranium is *G. sanguineum lancastriense* 'Splendens', rose-pink flowers, growing 25 cm (10 in) high and spreading to about 50 cm (20 in). *G.* 'Johnson's Blue' is a popular hybrid with cup-shaped

A selection of ground cover plants, including *Epimedium* in the foreground, *Euphorbia* at the back and *Hedera* on the wall.

lavender-blue flowers growing 30 cm (1 ft) high with a 60 cm (2 ft) spread; and the white-flowered *G. macrorrhizum* 'Album', of similar dimensions, is a good companion to it, and has particularly fragrant leaves. Rather larger-growing species are *G. phaeum*, with sprays of small maroon blooms, and *G. p.* 'Album', white. Some smaller forms, suitable for the front of borders or rockeries, growing about 25 cm (10 in) by 45 cm (1½ ft), include *G. pratense* 'Album' (syn. *G. rectum* 'Album'), white flowered; *G.* 'Russell Prichard', deep red; *G. sanguineum*, royal purple; *G. s. album*, white; and *G. s.* 'Splendens', pink, all with trailing, spreading stems. Propagate by division in autumn or spring.

Geum (avens)

Clump former. Deciduous. A cheerful genus of plants which produce bright-coloured flowers from early to late summer, and thick hairy leaves. All like sun and a well-drained soil, and height and spread are up to 30 cm (1 ft). They are particularly useful for the front of borders. Popular geums to grow are G. × *borisii*, bright orange; 'Coppertones', hanging coppery bell flowers; and 'Georgenberg', deep yellow. All geums tend to be somewhat short lived and are best propagated by spring division every few years.

Helleborus (hellebore)

Clump former. Evergreen or deciduous. Long-living plants which grow well in shade, particularly among shrubs, in a rich soil and produce long-lasting flowers in winter or early spring. The best forms to grow for ground cover purposes are the evergreens, with their deeply-lobed rich

Geranium macrorrhizum 'Album' is most attractive in a light woodland setting.

green leaves keeping weeds under control all year round. *Helleborus corsicus*, with apple-green flowers in late spring, reaches a height of about 60 cm (2 ft) and spreads 90 cm (3 ft) or more. *H. foetidus*, pale green blooms attractively set against dark green foliage in late winter, grows about 38 cm (15 in) high by 45 cm (1½ ft) spread, and *H. niger* (the Christmas rose), with white flushed pink blooms in winter, reaches about 23 cm (9 in) in height and spreads about 45 cm (1½ ft). The Lenten rose, *H. orientalis*, is evergreen in mild districts, semi-evergreen elsewhere; it produces its flowers, which may be white, pink, green or purplish according to the various coloured forms, early in the year and grows about 30 cm (1 ft) by 60 cm (2 ft). All are best propagated by raising new plants from summer-sown seed, as established plants resent disturbance.

Hemerocallis (day lily)

Clump former. Deciduous. With the introduction of a wide range of superb coloured hybrids, day lilies have become increasingly popular. Their long, arching, pale green grass-like foliage forms decorative and unusually shaped clumps in contrast to the growing habit of many plants. This makes them a feature point for shrubberies or borders. If the dead leaves are left on the plants in winter, they will continue to do their duty as weed smotherers. The flowers, which open one at a time per stem and last only a day, are produced successively for a long period during the summer, especially if a mixture of hybrids are planted. Day lilies grow well in any soil, in sun or light shade, and are generally very adaptable plants. Most of the hybrids available grow to a height and spread of between 60 and 90 cm (2 and 3 ft). Just a few from which to choose include 'Black Magic', deep red-purple with yellow centre; 'Bonanza', buff-yellow with brown throat; 'Golden Chimes', golden yellow; 'Hyperion', clear yellow and fragrant; 'Pink Damask', pink; and 'Stella d'Oro', canary-yellow with orange throat. Propagate by division between autumn and spring.

Heuchera (coral flower)

Clump former. Evergreen. With the introduction of modern hybrids and varieties, heucheras have become more popular as ground cover plants. Their evergreen, heart-shaped leaves form good clumps, or almost carpets if the plants are set close enough together. From these clumps, tall slender stems arise to bear clusters of brightly coloured flowers from early to mid-summer. The plants do best in good soil and sun, though they tolerate light shade. The height and spread of the leaves is about 15 cm (6 in) by 45 cm (1½ ft) and the height of the flower spikes varies between 45 cm (1½ ft) and 60 cm (2 ft). Good forms to select include 'Coral Cloud', coral red; 'Greenfinch', greenish yellow; 'Sheer Variety', scarlet; 'Palace Purple', purple leaves and white flowers; and 'Bressingham Hybrids', mixed colours. Propagate by division between autumn and spring or seed sown in spring. To keep the plants from becoming woody and straggly, it is advisable to divide every few years and replant the best of the young growth.

Hosta (syn. *Funkia*) (plantain lily)
Clump former. Deciduous. Hostas are grown as ground cover plants mainly for their decorative and dense leaf growth, with their stems of flower clusters as an added attraction in summer. They do well in almost any ground and situation but flourish in a fairly rich moist soil and are useful against north facing walls, among shrubs or other herbaceous plants. Most hosta leaves grow between 30 and 45 cm (1 and 1½ ft) tall and spread 45–60 cm (1½–2 ft), while the height of the flower spikes, with their lily-like blooms, is between 45 cm (1½ ft) and 90 cm (3 ft). There are many species and hybrids from which to choose and some of the most popular include *Hosta fortunei* 'Aurea', yellow to light green leaves, purple flowers; *H. f.* 'Albo Picta' (syn. 'Picta'), yellow and green leaves in spring, mauve flowers; *H. f.* 'Aurea Marginata', gold-edged leaves, mauve flowers; *H. sieboldiana* 'Bressingham Blue', glaucous blue leaves, white flowers; *H. ventricosa* 'Variegata', dark leaves edged cream, deep blue flowers; *H.* 'Frances Williams', glaucous leaves with beige markings, pale mauve flowers; *H.* 'Francee', rich green white-edged leaves, pale mauve flowers; and *H.* 'Shade Fanfare', cream-edged leaves, lavender-blue flowers. Propagate by division in spring.

Houttuynia
Spreader. Deciduous. *Houttuynia cordata* 'Flore Pleno' is a good ground coverer for damp, boggy places. Its purple-shaded heart-shaped leaves smell of oranges and cone-like clusters of white flowers are produced in summer. Its height and spread are about 15 cm (6 in) by 60 cm (2 ft). Propagate by division in spring.

Iberis (candytuft)
Carpeter. Evergreen. The perennial iberis (see Chapter 7 for annual varieties) is sometimes listed under shrubs or alpines but is more usually treated as an herbaceous plant. Most frequently grown is *Iberis sempervirens* and its variety 'Snowflake', which are ideal for walls, rockeries and containers and are particularly useful in town gardens. They like plenty of sun and a well-drained soil, and in such positions form mounds of evergreen leaves which become covered with showy white flowers in summer. The average height is about 23 cm (9 in) and spread can be up to 90 cm (3 ft). Propagate by soft wood cuttings or layering in summer.

Lamium (dead nettle)

Carpeter. Evergreen, or nearly so. Dead nettles are ideal ground cover plants in shrubberies, under trees, on banks or in a naturalized area, but most species and varieties are too invasive for small gardens or herbaceous borders. They grow well in any soil and tolerate sun or shade. Most commonly grown is *Lamium* (syn. *Lamiastrum*) *galeobdolon* 'Variegatum', yellow archangel, with its silver and green variegated leaves which turn bronze in winter and early summer yellow flowers. Its height is about 30 cm (1 ft) and spread can ultimately be 2.7 m (9 ft) or more, though initially young plants should be planted about 45 cm ($1\frac{1}{2}$ ft) apart. Varieties of *L. maculatum*, such as 'Beacon Silver', silvery white leaves and pink flowers, and 'Roseum', with a white central stripe in the leaves and clear pink blooms, are particularly useful as more compact carpeters that grow rapidly. Their height and spread is about 30 cm (1 ft) by 90 cm (3 ft). Propagate by division in autumn or spring.

Hosta (plantain lily) species and hybrids, with their various leaf colours, make useful ground cover plants.

Iberis umbellata varieties are colourful hardy annuals for weed suppression.

Liriope

Clump former. Evergreen. Grassy shiny-leaved plants which are excellent in borders and among shrubs, liriopes grow best in well drained, lime-free soil in a sunny position, though they will tolerate light shade. The most suitable species is *Liriope muscari* which forms hummocks up to 30 cm (1 ft) high with a spread of 45 cm (1½ ft), its leaves giving all-year-round ground cover. In late summer and autumn tall spikes of violet bell shaped flowers are produced. Propagate by division in spring.

Lysichitum

Clump forming. Deciduous. Where space permits and large oramental plants are required for a moist boggy soil or side of a stream, in either sun or shade, the two forms of lysichitum are excellent. Both grow to a height and spread of up to 1.2 m (4 ft). The flowers are borne in the spring before the large handsome leaves appear; the blooms of *Lysichitum americanum* are like bright yellow scrolls and have an offensive smell, whereas those of *L. camtschatcensis* are fragrant, white and arum lily-like in appearance. Propagate from self-sown seedlings or by division in spring.

Lysimachia (creeping jenny)

Carpeter. Evergreen. Although there are a number of lysimachias suitable for growing in moist soil in the garden, and which will help suppress weeds, *Lysimachia nummularia* and its variety *L. m.* 'Aurea' are excellent dense ground coverers for carpeting old unsightly walls, wet banks, the damp areas around ornamental pools and in any wet situation in the garden. They like sun or light shade. Both have rounded leaves borne on creeping stems (those of *L. m.* 'Aurea' are yellow) and bear yellow flowers in mid-summer. Height is about 5 cm (2 in) and spread up to about 60 cm (2 ft). *L. punctata*, yellow loosestrife, grows taller and is very invasive, so is particularly useful for semi-wild areas; its spires of bright yellow flowers are most attractive. Propagate by division between autumn and spring.

Nepeta (catmint)

Clump former. Evergreen, or nearly so. The best of the catmints for ground cover purposes is *Nepeta* × *faassenii* (syn. *N. mussinii*) which is excellent for edging, dry walls or containers. Its silvery fern-like leaves and spikes of lavender-mauve flowers in summer make it an attractive addition to any garden. It grows in well-drained soil in a sunny position and, to prevent it dying out in the centre, should be cut over with shears in spring or after flowering. Its height and spread are about 30–45 cm (1–1½ ft). 'Blue Beauty' is another recent introduction suitable for ground cover purposes, and grows to the same height and spread; it has lavender-blue spikes. It can become invasive. Propagate by division in spring.

Oxalis

Carpeter or clump former. Evergreen or deciduous. Not unlike the shamrock, all have clover-like leaves, which fold in an attractive manner when not in full light, and produce pink or white flowers in early to mid-summer. Some grow best in rich well-drained soils in shade, others in well-drained soil in sun, but care must be taken with those with invasive bulbous rootstocks not to allow them to swamp other low growing plants. The various species are useful plants for rockeries, woodland, shrubberies or containers. If you can obtain it, *Oxalis oregana* is the best for shady positions and its roots are not invasive; its height is about 15 cm (6 in), spread about 90 cm (3 ft), and the flowers pink. *O. magellanica* is another good species, with bronze-coloured leaves and white flowers forming an attractive carpet. It grows about 5 cm (2 in) high but slowly spreads to 30 cm (12 in) or thereabouts. Two bulbous species, growing particularly well in hot, dry spots, are O. *adenophylla*, grey leaves and pink flowers, and O. *inops*, light green foliage and pink blooms. Both grow about 10 cm (4 in) tall and spread about 30 cm (1 ft), but they increase themselves freely and generally require control by weeding to prevent them spreading farther than required. Propagate by division of the rootstock or bulbs in spring.

Phlomis (Jerusalem sage)
Carpeter. Evergreen or deciduous. Phlomis are tallish growing plants which are ideal for herbaceous or mixed borders which get plenty of sun. The evergreen *Phlomis fruticosa* with its woolly grey-green leaves makes an excellent foil for other plants and it produces yellow flowers in early summer. Its height and spread are about 90 cm (3 ft). Equally attractive are *P. russeliana* (syn. *P. viscosa*) and *P. samia*. *P. russeliana* has large, wrinkled hairy leaves and clusters of yellow flowers in early summer. *P. samia* is purple. Their height and spread are about 90 cm (3ft). Propagate by late summer cuttings of *P. fruticosa* and division of the other two in autumn and spring.

Phlox
Carpeter. Deciduous. The tall growing phlox are unsuitable for ground coverers, but the varieties and hybrids of *Phlox douglasii* and *P. subulata* are excellent and reliable plants for rockeries, stone walls, front of borders or containers. All those listed are free-flowering, long-lived, and make an attractive colour scheme when different coloured varieties are planted to create a mass effect. They all require fertile, well-drained soil in full sun to form attractive mats of tiny, thin leaves and produce masses of flowers in early summer. In general, all the dwarf forms available reach a height of about 8 cm (3 in), with flower heads on 8–15 cm (3–6 in) stems, and spread about 45 cm (1½ ft). Some good forms to choose include 'Daniels Cushion', rose-pink; 'Eva', mauve; 'May Snow', pure white; 'Red Admiral', crimson; 'Waterloo', ruby-crimson; 'Oakington Blue', sky blue; 'Scarlet Flame', scarlet; 'Temiscaming', deep rose; and 'White Delight', pure white. Propagate by division in autumn or spring or by summer basal cuttings.

Polygonum (knotweed)
Carpeter or clump former. Deciduous. There are a number of knotweeds suitable for ground covering. With the exception of *Polygonum vaccinifolium,* an 8 cm (3 in) tall and 60 cm (2 ft) spreading plant with pink

Lysimachia nummularia (creeping jenny) forms excellent evergreen ground cover for damp sites.

flowers in late summer, which requires a sunny well-drained soil such as in a rockery, the others mentioned will all grow well in sun or partial shade, provided the soil is moist but not waterlogged. One of the most popular knotweeds is *Polygonum affine* 'Darjeeling Red', which has carpet-forming leaves which remain brown in winter and spikes of dense deep pink flowers for several months in late summer. It grows only 8 cm (3 in) tall, though the flower spikes reach up to 25 cm (10 in) and spreads about 60 cm (2 ft); it is thus suitable for the front of borders or in rock gardens. The smaller variety *P.a.* 'Dimity' is also popular, with its shorter pink flower 'pokers' and very colourful autumn foliage which also lasts through the winter until fresh leaf growth appears in spring. Two taller sturdy clump-forming species, suitable for borders or banks near streams, are *P. campanulatum,* 60 cm (2 ft) by 90 cm (3 ft), with rosettes of grooved leaves and long-lasting spikes of pink flowers, and *P. amplexi-caule,* 1.2 m (4 ft) tall and wide, with large dark green leaves and flower spikes from summer to late autumn, which are deep red in the variety *P.a.* 'Atrosanguineum' and crimson in *P.a.* 'Firetail'. Propagate by division in autumn or early spring.

Potentilla (cinquefoil)
Carpeter or clump former. Deciduous. Some of the herbaceous potentillas (see Chapter 9 for the shrub forms) make excellent ground cover plants suitable for borders, rockeries, walls or containers. All prefer sun and well-drained soil and will flower for a long period in summer. Two neat little carpet-forming species for the rock garden or walls are *Potentilla alba*, white flowers, and *P. verna* (syn. *P. tabernaemontani*) 'Nana', yellow flowers. Both grow about 8 cm (3 in) tall and spread about 30 cm (1 ft).

Sedum kamtschaticum 'Variegatum' (stonecrop) produces golden flowers above its evergreen leaves.

Among the larger forms suitable for borders are *P. argyrophylla*, with silvery grey leaves and crimson flowers, and numerous hybrids, of which 'Gibson's Scarlet', with bright red blooms with almost black centres, is one of the most popular as it retains a neat habit of growth. Other good hybrids, also with silver-grey leaves, include 'Flamenco', red; 'Firedance', shades of red; and 'William Rollison', orange and yellow. The annual *P. recta warrenii* is more erect, produces golden-yellow flowers and forms an attractive plant. All grow 30–40 cm (12–15 in) high and spread up to 60 cm (2 ft). Propagate by division in autumn or spring, basal cuttings in spring or seed sown in spring.

Prunella (self-heal)

Carpeter. Evergreen. Self-heal make excellent ground covers for the front of herbaceous or mixed borders where the soil is moist; they are equally happy in sun or light shade. They can become invasive by self-sown seedlings, and to keep them under control it is advisable to remove dead flower heads. They all have rather broad, dark green leaves and for a long period in summer produce spikes of dead-nettle like flowers in various colours. *P. × webbiana,* which grows about 30 cm (1 ft) by about 60 cm (2 ft), has rosy purple blooms. Most commonly grown, however, are the varieties 'Loveliness', lilac; 'Loveliness Pink', clear pink; and 'Loveliness White', pure white, all of which have a height and spread of about 15 cm (6 in) by 45 cm ($1\frac{1}{2}$ ft). 'Little Red Riding Hood' (syn. 'Rotkäppchen'), with crimson-pink flowers is smaller and has a less spreading habit than the others mentioned, which makes it particularly useful in the rock garden. Propagate by division in autumn or early spring.

Pulmonaria (lungwort)
Clump former. Deciduous or evergreen. All lungworts are very easily grown and make effective cover anywhere where the soil can be kept moist in summer, be it in sun or shade. They are particularly useful against north-facing walls, in shrubberies or woodland areas, and their late spring flowers make them a welcome addition to any garden. *Pulmonaria angustifolia* deciduous varieties include 'Munstead Blue', rich blue, and 'Mrs Moon', rose-pink, both with green, grey-spotted lance-shaped leaves, which die back to a central crown in winter. Generally more popular are the evergreen lungworts with their large green or silvery green hairy leaves spotted or mottled white. Popular ground coverers are varieties of *P. saccharata* (syn. *P. picta*), such as 'Sissinghurst White'; 'Argentea', blue; 'Bowles Red'; 'Highdown', sky-blue; and 'Pink Dawn', rose-pink. All grow to a height of 15–30 cm (6–12 in) and spread 30 cm (1 ft) or more. Propagate by division in autumn or early spring.

Saponaria (soapwort, bouncing bet)
Carpeter. Evergreen. Only two forms are commonly grown and these do best as edgings to borders, in the rockery or trailing down walls or banks. They like a sunny position and a well-drained soil. *Saponaria* 'Bressingham Hybrid' is perhaps the most attractive, with pink white-eyed flowers in early summer rising above a carpet of small, hairy, bright green leaves; its height and spread are 5 cm (2 in) by 15 cm (6 in) or more. *S. ocymoides* is a more vigorous plant, growing 8 cm (3 in) high but trailing about 60 cm (2 ft), and it produces a wealth of pink flower clusters from mid to late summer. Propagate by division in autumn or early spring.

Saxifraga (saxifrage)
Carpeter. Evergreen. Saxifrages are particularly valuable for growing in rock gardens or among paving stones, with some of the larger forms being suitable for edging borders or growing in containers. They form a rather complex genus and are usually divided into four main sections, from which a choice of species and varieties can be made according to the planting sites in mind. For ground cover purposes the 'Mossy' (*Dactyloides*) saxifrage hybrids are to be recommended for, as their name implies, they form mossy carpets of small leaves from which spikes of dainty flowers appear in late spring and early summer. They all like a certain amoung of shade and a soil which is not too dry. Their average height is 8 cm (3 in) and spread about 30 cm (1 ft). Among the many good forms are 'Dartington Double', double pink; 'Flowers of Sulphur', sulphur-yellow; 'Gaiety', deep rose-pink; 'Cloth of Gold', golden leaves and white flowers; 'Pearly King', white; 'Pixie', rose-red; and 'Triumph',

blood red. Various other saxifrages with carpeting foliage are *Saxifraga cuneifolia,* white, 5 cm (2 in) by 30 cm (1 ft); *S. umbrosa* (syn. *S. urbium*) (London Pride), mats of rosettes of leaves with pink starry flowers on long stalks, 30 cm (1 ft) by 45 cm (1½ ft); *S. u. primuloides* 'Elliott's Variety', a smaller London Pride, and 'Variegata', similar in size and colour to London Pride but with attractive yellow-splashed leaves. All these also like a semi-shady position and a well-drained but not too dry soil. They are all good as border edging plants. Propagate by division after flowering.

Sedum (stonecrop)

Clump former or carpeter. Evergreen or deciduous. All stonecrops like plenty of sun and grow best in rough but well-drained soil. Some species and varieties are suitable for borders while others are best confined to walls or the rockery. Flowering time ranges over a long period during the summer, and butterflies are always attracted to the brightly coloured heads of blooms. Equally, the various leaf forms give added attraction. Some suitable ground coverers for borders include *Sedum roseum* (now *rhodiola*) which is deciduous, has grey-green leaves up a thick stem, yellowish green flower heads in early summer, and grows to a height and spread of about 30 cm (12 in); *S.* × 'Ruby Glow', deciduous, blue-green fleshy leaves, brilliant rose-red flowers in late summer, 30 cm (12 in) by 30 cm (12 in); *S. spectabile,* deciduous, large, fleshy, greyish leaves, light pink flower heads in early autumn, up to 45 cm (1½ ft) in height and spread; and *S. s.* 'Autumn Joy', deciduous, large, fleshy blue-green leaves, pink deepening to orange-brown flowers in large heads in autumn, about 45 cm (1½ ft) by 60 cm (2 ft). These are all clump formers, but an unusual evergreen carpeting sedum, which bears no flowers but makes an excellent foil for bulbs, small trees or shrubs, is *S. spurium* 'Green Mantle', which grows only 8 cm (3 in) high but spreads up to 60 cm (2 ft).

For walls, rock gardens, paved areas, raised patio beds, or for growing in a variety of containers, the following, which grow about 10 cm (4 in) by 30 cm (1 ft), are but some of the wide number of sedums available: *S. kamtschaticum* 'Variegatum', evergreen, bright green variegated leaves, golden mid-summer flower heads; *S. spathulifolium,* evergreen, mat-forming rosettes of grey-green leaves, bright yellow flowers in early summer (*S. s.* 'Cappa Blanca' has grey-white leaves and yellow flowers, and *S. s.* 'Purpureum', has broad purple leaves and yellow flowers). *S. spurium* 'Purple Carpet', with evergreen carpets of purple-red leaves, produces rosy red flowers in mid-summer and grows in a similar habit reaching 8 cm (3 in) by 60 cm (2 ft). Propagate by division between autumn and spring.

Stachys (lamb's ear, lamb's tail)
Carpeter. Evergreen. The low-growing species and its varieties most usually grown do well in a sunny position in free-draining soil. *Stachys lanata* (syn. *S. olympica*), is more commonly grown for its curious spreading habit and white woolly leaves; it produces spikes of purple flowers in mid-summer and grows about 30 cm (12 in) by 30 cm (12 in). Its variety *S. l.* 'Silver Carpet' is shorter and forms good ground cover and a neat edging plant but is non-flowering. *S. l.* 'Sheila MacQueen' has larger leaves and silvery flower spikes in mid-summer and reaches the same proportions as the species. All three are useful as front of border plants for all year round attraction. Another vigorous ground covering species is *S. byzantina,* rather larger than 'Silver Carpet' with bold woolly foliage and deep pink flower spikes; it grows particularly well in dry, sunny positions. Propagate by division between autumn and spring.

Symphytum (comfrey)
Carpeter or clump former. Evergreen. A very useful genus for quick growing ground cover plants which will do well in almost any situation, including moist soils and under trees. They are particularly suitable plants for wild gardens, light woodland or in shrubberies. The smaller of the two most popular species is *Symphytum grandiflorum,* growing about 23 cm (9 in) tall and spreading up to 60 cm (2 ft). It has large hairy leaves and produces tubular creamy white flowers in late spring. Its varieties, 'Hidcote Blue' and 'Hidcote Pink', produce pale blue and pale pink flowers respectively which are borne on longer stems than the species. A bigger plant altogether, and clump forming, which is more suitable for large gardens, is *S.* × *uplandicum* (sometimes listed as *S. peregrinum*) and its variegated leaf form *S.* × *u.* 'Variegatum'. Height and spread are about 90 cm (3 ft) and the flower colours are purple-blue and lilac-pink respectively. Propagate by division in autumn or spring.

Tellima
Clump former. Evergreen. *Tellima grandiflora* and its variety *T. g.* 'Purpurea' (with bronze leaves) are excellent evergreen ground coverers for shaded borders, shrubberies, light woodland, north-facing wall borders and in town gardens. Their leaves form good soil-covering clumps with a height and spread of 30 cm (1 ft) by about 60 cm (2 ft) and in late spring tallish stems of cream-yellow bell-shaped flowers are produced. Propagate by division between autumn and spring.

Thymus (thyme)
Carpeter. Evergreen. Thymes may be classed either as herbaceous perennials or as shrubs, but are most often listed as herbaceous or herb plants. Described here are all cultivated forms of the wild thyme and, as such,

Veronica teucrium (speedwell) is an ideal weed smotherer in herbaceous borders.

grow best in free-draining soil which gets plenty of sun – they will even withstand drought conditions. They are ideal for rockeries or between paving. All have small aromatic evergreen leaves which, in some cases, may be grey and woolly, and the mid-summer flowers are usually pink, sometimes white. Most widely grown are the varieties of *Thymus serpyllum* (more correctly called *T. drucei*) such as 'Albus', 'Annie Hall', 'Coccineus', 'Lanuginosus' and 'Pink Chintz'. A very attractive little carpeter with greyish foliage is *T. doefleri*. 'Anderson's Gold' is a very dwarf carpeter and has bright golden foliage all the year round. All grow about 5 cm (2 in) high and spread 60 cm (2 ft) or more. Propagate by division in spring or late summer. (All mentioned can be used instead of grass for lawn-like areas – see Chapter 6.)

Tiarella (foam flower)
Carpeter. Evergreen. *Tiarella cordifolia* is both highly decorative and an efficient ground coverer for semi-shady positions in shrub borders or wild gardens where the soil has plenty of humus and remains moist. It has three-lobed green leaves, turning a bronze colour in winter, carried on surface stems and in early summer produces spikes of creamy white flowers. The foliage grows about 8 cm (3 in) high and spreads 60 cm (2 ft) or more. Propagate by division in autumn or spring.

Trollius (globe flower)
Clump former. Deciduous. For those with heavy, moist or boggy soils, or where cover planting along streams or around pools is required, globe flowers are most useful; they will grow well in sun or semi-shade. Their double, yellow or orange buttercup-like flowers in late spring and deeply divided rich green leaves are always decorative from early spring to early winter. Most popular are the hybrids of *Trollius × hybridus*, such as 'Golden Queen', 'Orange Princess' and 'Gold Cup'. Overall height is 30–60 cm (1–2 ft) and spread 45–60 cm (1½–2 ft). Propagate by division in autumn or spring.

Veronica (speedwell)
Clump former or carpeter. Deciduous or evergreen. Speedwells are easily grown plants in a well drained soil where they get plenty of sun. There are species and varieties suitable both for the border or rockery; the border varieties are clump formers whereas the smaller ones are carpeters. For borders, *Veronica gentianoides,* with its clumps of basal leaves forming rosettes and its tall spikes of powder-blue in spring, makes a pretty sight; the height and spread of the foliage is about 30 cm (1 ft). The creamy white leaved *V. g.* 'Variegata' is smaller and makes a useful edging plant. Also similar in height and spread are *V. teucrium* and its varieties 'Crater Lake Blue', 'Shirley Blue' and 'Trehane', all with blue flowers. In the

rock garden, *V. prostrata* (*V. rupestris* of gardens) and its varieties, such as 'Blue Sheen', 'Loddon Blue' and 'Spode Blue', are most commonly grown. All have green leaves and small spikes of blue flowers which smother the plants in early summer; height and spead are 10–15 cm (4–6 in) by 30–45 cm (1–1½ ft). Vigorous-growing carpeters with grey-green leaves and blue flowers in summer are *V. cinerea* and *V. pectinata* 'Rosea', similar to the former but with pink instead of blue flowers. Propagate by division in spring.

Viola (pansy)

Carpeter. Evergreen. Although there are many species and varieties of pansies, only a few of the evergreen species are suitable ground coverers. They like open positions where the soil is moist but not waterlogged, and are excellent for rockeries, edging or as a carpet under roses. They grow about 8–10 cm (3–4 in) tall and spread about 30–45 cm (1–1½ ft). Their small leaves, usually dark green, and pansy-like flowers appearing from spring to autumn, make them attractive all-year-round plants. Good species to grow are *Viola cornuta,* lilac-purple; *V. c.* 'Boughton Blue', light blue; *V. labradorica,* purplish leaves and lavender-blue flowers (this species will also grow well in shade); and *V. gracilis* 'Lutea', canary-yellow. Other suitable violas include 'Ardross Gem', light blue flushed with gold; 'Clementine', true violet-blue; and 'Nora Leigh', pale violet-blue. Propagate by summer basal cuttings or seed sown in spring or summer, or by autumn division.

Waldsteinia

Carpeter. Evergreen. *Waldsteinia ternata* is a versatile ground coverer growing well in most types of soil and in sun or shade. It forms mats of thick dark green evergreen foliage and produces strawberry-like yellow flower sprays in spring. Its height and spread are approximately 10 cm (4 in) by 60 cm (2 ft), so it is best planted where it can spread freely, such as in large rockeries, shrubberies, light woodland or wild garden areas. Propagate by division in autumn or spring.

CHAPTER 9

SHRUBS

As the desire for labour-saving gardens increases, so shrubs which require little maintenance have come to play a more important role in general planning and landscaping. Furthermore, it is often cheaper to stock one's garden with carefully selected shrubs, most of which will live for a great many years, than it is to buy and plant at regular intervals short-lived herbaceous perennials or bedding plants twice a year. These latter two groups of plants do have their parts to play in many cases but, when it comes to permanency and little attention, shrubs are hard to better.

Shrubs, including the dwarf and slow-growing conifers (little evergreen 'trees' with tiny scale-, awl- or needle-like leaves and inconspicuous flowers sometimes followed by cones or berries), are those plants which have woody stems and branches but no single main trunks as do trees. They can be very low growing or prostrate, or much larger and of more rounded form. They can be deciduous (lose their leaves in winter) or be evergreen (keep their leaves all year round).

Obviously, when choosing shrubs for ground cover purposes the evergreen forms are likely to prove most popular. Not only do they do their job of making the garden look furnished at every season of the year but they also suppress weeds all the time. However, there are some deciduous shrubs included in this chapter which, because of their habit of growth and vigour, are very nearly as effective as weed suppressors as are evergreens.

It is quite possible in a small garden to make a very effective sight with only a carefully selected collection of shrubs, perhaps with a few bulbs for additional spring colour at low level. The shrubs can be chosen to present different growth forms and leaf colour as well as blending or contrasting with each other at different eye levels. Equally, many of the shrubs described can be grown in containers, in soil pockets on patios, or in retaining walls and rock gardens. Many of the shrubs in the following lists are suitable for just these purposes and offer a labour-saving form of interesting gardening, especially if one chooses unusual species, varieties and hybrids.

In larger gardens, the scope for selecting ground covering shrubs is considerable, and there are plenty which will fit in well with existing shrubberies, mixed borders, light woodland, wild areas or create weed-free screening hedges or hide unsightly objects such as manhole covers, compost areas and so on.

Some shrubs grow relatively quickly but others are slower and hand weeding may be required for the first year or so. Alternatively, black polythene sheeting can be put around the young plants to suppress weeds and then be moved as the plants mature.

In the following lists, the heights and spreads given for each plant are average figures as obviously growing conditions can alter the final sizes. Equally, the spread normally indicates the distance at which to position the young plants.

Indication as to the method of growth of the shrubs is given, i.e. whether they are carpeters, spreaders, hummocks or sprawlers, and the definition of these terms is given on pp.8–9. Also brief notes on pruning and propagating are included, as well as suggestions for siting the plants, in sun or shade and the type of soil required. Unless otherwise specified, the shrubs are all hardy.

Aucuba (spotted laurel)

Hummock. Evergreen. Although a common plant, it is extremely versatile, growing in any situation and soil, including deep shade, and its large shiny green or variegated evergreen foliage makes it a good ground coverer. It is even suitable for container growing. The flowers are inconspicuous but, if both male and female forms (one male to up to ten females) are grown, clusters of red berries are produced in autumn. *Aucuba japonica*, ultimate height and spread 1.5 m (5 ft), is the most common form, and its varieties with yellow and green leaves, such as *A. j.* 'Maculata' and *A. j.* 'Picturata' are attractive variations. *A. j.* 'Nana Rotundifolia' is a somewhat smaller, rich green-leaved, female form. Other good varieties are 'Crotonifolia' (male), golden variegated leaves; 'Lance Leaf' (male), deep green; and the females 'Gold Dust', golden-blotched foliage, and 'Longifolia', bright green. Prune if necessary in spring. Propagate by summer heel cuttings.

Azalea (See *Rhododendron*)

Berberis (barberry)

Hummock. Evergreen. This is a large and popular genus of plants for many purposes, but for ground covering the evergreen species, hybrids and varieties are the most useful. Barberries will grow in any except waterlogged soil and do well in sun or light shade. Most are spiny, have dark green, glossy, rather small leaves, and produce yellow or orange flowers in abundance in spring, sometimes followed by berries. Good forms to grow include *Berberis* × *bristolensis* which has holly-like leaves, white beneath, and reaches about 60 cm (2 ft) in height but spreads densely to about 1.2 m (4 ft). *B. candidula* is somewhat similar, with the addition of black-purple berries in summer, which has a height and spread of 45 cm (1½ ft) by about 1.2 m (4 ft). *B. c.* 'Amstelveen' has a dense habit and grows faster than the species, to reach a height and spread of about 90 cm (3 ft), while *B. c.* 'Telstar', with lighter green leaves, grows about 75 cm (2½ ft) by 1.2 m (4 ft). *B. calliantha* is again somewhat like *B.* × *bristolensis*, but with red stems, which reaches 90 cm (3 ft) by 90 cm (3 ft). Another dense and compact form is *B. hookeri*, with yellow flowers and purple berries and a height and spread of about 90 cm (3 ft). A slow-growing handsome form with arching stems is *B. verruculosa*, ultimately reaching a height and spread of 1–1½ m (3¼–5 ft) with glossy leaves with a white under surface, which often colour in autumn, and yellow flowers followed by black berries. Although not strictly ever-green, *B. wilsonae* often holds its densely placed bluish green leaves until mid-winter, when its red and orange autumn colours look splendid with the clusters of orange-red fruits. Its thorny arching stems make it ideal for covering banks. Prune if necessary after flowering. Propagate by autumn heel cuttings, or divide if rooted sucker shoots are present, between autumn and winter.

Calluna (heather, ling) (See *Erica*)

Ceanothus
Hummock. Evergreen. Although there are a number of deciduous species and hybrids, for ground cover purposes the evergreen forms are far more useful. Unfortunately, they are not in the main as hardy as the deciduous types, but in warm areas, especially where in sheltered sunny positions, they will grow freely. If in doubt about the hardiness of young plants, it is a wise precaution to protect them during the winter months with sacking, bracken or straw. Two truly hardy forms which add visual impact to any shrub border with their flower spikes of varying shades of blue in late spring and early summer are *Ceanothus* × *burkwoodii*, with a height and spread of 2–3 m (6½–10 ft), and *C. thyrsiflorus* 'Repens', height about 1 m (3¼ ft) and spread about 2 m (6½ ft). The former has a somewhat arching growth habit and leaves that are shiny green above and grey below. The latter grows very quickly, has dark green glossy leaves, a wealth of smaller fluffy flowerheads and is particularly suitable for a large rockery or sunny bank. All ceanothus will grow well in a sunny position where the soil is free-draining but has a high humus con-tent; none of them likes chalky soils and annual peat dressings are an advantage. Pruning is usually unnecessary. Propagate by side-shoot cuttings in summer.

Cistus (rock rose)
Hummock. Evergreen. Rock roses are not always fully hardy in all parts
of the country but several species and hybrids grow well if planted in
light well-drained soil, a sunny position, and where they are sheltered
from frosts and cold north and east winds. They are also good ground
coverers for maritime areas, and give of their best in rock gardens, on
walls or dry banks. Their evergreen leaves form a good permanent carpet
against weeds and their masses of wild-rose-like flowers in summer and
early autumn smother the bushes. Among the hardiest of rock roses are
Cistus × corbariensis, with pointed wavy-edged green leaves and red
flower buds opening white, which has a height and spread of about 1½ m
(5 ft); *C. × lusitanicus* 'Decumbens', dark green leaves, white, brown-
spotted flowers, height about 45 cm (1½ ft) and spread up to 1.2 m (4 ft);
C. laurifolius, leathery, large, tapering leaves, large white flowers with
yellow centre and height and spread about 90 cm (3 ft); and *C.* 'Silver
Pink', silvery leaves, soft pink crinkled flowers, height and spread about
90 cm (3 ft). Other forms may well grow satisfactorily in your garden
though growth could be killed by frosts, in which case this should be cut
out in spring; otherwise no pruning is necessary. Propagate by seed sown
in spring or side-shoot cuttings in summer.

Convolvulus
Hummock. Evergreen. Most people associate convolvulus with climbing
plants and the strangling weed so often encountered, but one shrubby
species, *Convolvulus cneorum*, is a pretty, hardy little evergreen ground
coverer. Its mass of narrow leaves are covered with silky hairs which
gives the bush a silvery appearance and it produces pink-budded white
trumpet-shaped flowers from summer to autumn. It grows well in a
sunny position in well-drained good soil, particularly in a rockery or
against a south facing wall. Its average height and spread is 60 cm (2 ft).
To keep the plant looking at its best, covering it with a cloche in winter
preserves its silvery appearance. No pruning is necessary. Propagate by
side-shoot heel cuttings in summer.

Cornus (syn. *Chamaepericlymenum*) (creeping dogwood)
Spreader. Deciduous. *Cornus canadensis* is the only member of the
dogwoods that is suitable for ground covering efficiently. It is more
herbaceous-like than shrubby, throwing up 15 cm (6 in) shoots from
underground creeping stems each spring, which spread about 60 cm
(2 ft). It grows well in light shade, such as a shrubbery or light woodland,
and does best in soil enriched with leaf mould or humus, is not chalky,
and which does not dry out. It has leaves in fours, which are dull green to
start with but tend to turn reddish in autumn and remain on the plants

until the first frosts. White flowers are produced in summer, often followed by berries in autumn. No pruning is required. Propagate by division in late autumn.

Cotoneaster

Hummock or carpeter. Evergreen, deciduous or semi-evergreen. Cotoneasters are an invaluable genus for a multitude of uses in the garden; they grow well in any soil and any position and are available in a variety of shapes and sizes. Some make excellent ground coverers, particularly useful for rock gardens, unsightly banks or walls, or for underplanting in shrubberies and woodland areas. The evergreen forms lend interest and shape to the garden all year and the deciduous species and varieties give a spell of bright foliage colours in autumn. Small white flowers are borne in early summer, and are often followed by brightly coloured red fruits, which last well into winter. Among the most popular and suitable evergreen ground coverers are: *Cotoneaster congestus*, slow growing but neat and effective, growing about 8 cm (3 in) high and spreading up to 45 cm ($1\frac{1}{2}$ ft); *C. conspicuus*, which is large and forms dense hummocks – 2 m ($6\frac{1}{2}$ ft) by 4 m (13 ft) or more – and suitable for unsightly banks or wild areas, and its smaller form *C. c.* 'Decorus', which grows about 1 m (3 ft) by 1.5 m (5 ft); *C. dammeri* makes a neat carpeter only 10 cm (4 in) high with a spread of about 60 cm (2 ft); *C.* 'Hybridus Pendulus', almost evergreen with arching branches, 30 cm (1 ft) high spreading 2 m ($6\frac{1}{2}$ ft) or so; *C. microphyllus* which forms a dense carpet about 45 cm ($1\frac{1}{2}$ ft) high by 1.5 m (5 ft) wide; *C. salicifolius* 'Autumn Fire', very strong growing with unusual willow-like leaves which are greyish beneath, has a height and spread of about 30 cm (1 ft) by 3.5 m ($11\frac{1}{2}$ ft); and *C.* 'Skogholm' (sometimes called 'Skogholm Coral Beauty' or just 'Coral Beauty' because of its deep coral-coloured fruits) which forms a dense cover about 30 cm (1 ft) high by 2.5 m ($8\frac{1}{4}$ ft) wide. The most widely-grown deciduous form is the fish-bone cotoneaster, *C. horizontalis*, with its fan-shaped flat-growing branches and brightly coloured leaves and fruits in autumn making a striking plant about 45 cm ($1\frac{1}{2}$ ft) high and 3 m (10 ft) wide. Its form *C. h.* 'Variegatus' has white edged leaves and does not grow as large. Prune back in early spring if the plants outgrow their alloted area. Propagate by heel cuttings in summer or layering in late autumn.

Cytisus (broom)

Hummock or carpeter. Deciduous. Brooms are free-flowering shrubs producing a wealth of pea-shaped blooms in late spring or early summer. They do not retain their leaves for a long period but those forms suitable as ground coverers create such a mass of branches that they form good

Cotoneaster horizontalis is a striking ground cover plant and makes a good feature in selected positions.

weed suppressors once established (hand weeding may be required during the first year or two). All like a position in full sun and prefer a sandy soil. The low-growing forms mentioned here are suitable for borders, walls or rockeries. *Cytisus* × *beanii* has yellow flowers and forms a hummock about 30 cm (1 ft) by 60 cm (2 ft); *C.* × *kewensis* has grey-green leaves, yellow flowers and is more spreading in habit, forming a carpet of about 1.2 m (4 ft); and *C. purpureus* has dark grey leaves, soft mauve blooms, and grows about 45 cm (1½ ft) by 1.2 m (4 ft). Prune if necessary after flowering. Propagate by heel cuttings in summer.

Daboecia (Irish heath, St Daboec's heath) (See *Erica*)

Erica (heath)
Hummock or carpeter. Evergreen. As all the heaths, heathers and lings are very similar, the three genera of *Calluna*, *Daboecia* and *Erica* are grouped together here. All, except the tree forms, make superb ground covering plants and they are equally attractive just in leaf as well as in flower, as both the small needle-like foliage and the bell-shaped flowers come in a variety of colours. By a careful selection of species, varieties and hybrids it is almost possible to have some in flower during every month of the year. With the exception of *Erica carnea*, *E. mediterranea* (syn. *E. erigena*, *E. hibernica*) and *E.* × *darleyensis* and their varieties and hybrids, which are lime tolerant, all other heaths and heathers require an

acid peaty soil. This can be created artificially by making special peat beds if required and by watering regularly each year with Sequestrene to supply the necessary nutrients for healthy growth. All like an open sunny position and a reasonably damp soil with plenty of humus, such as would be found in their native moorlands. They are best grown on their own, though it is becoming popular these days to create mixed beds of dwarf and slow-growing conifers with heaths and heathers to provide all-year-round attractive and labour-saving features. All the good ground covering forms grow to a height and spread of about 15–60 cm (6–24 in) and for best effect it is advisable to plant them in groups of at least three or more.

Prune away dead heads of summer and autumn-flowering forms in spring, and winter and spring ones after flowering. Propagate by layering or side-shoot cuttings in late summer.

Winter and spring flowering forms. Useful to choose from are *Erica carnea* 'December Red'; 'King George', rose-pink; 'Praecox Rubra', rose red; 'Aurea', deep pink with golden leaves; 'Springwood White'; 'Springwood Pink'; and 'Vivellii', carmine with bronze winter leaves; *E. × darleyensis* 'Arthur Johnson', pink; 'Ghost Hills, deep pink, cream-tipped young growths; 'Darley Dale', pink; 'Furzey', deep pink; 'Silber-schmelze' (syns. 'Silver Beads' and 'Molten Silver'), white; and *E. mediterranea* (syn. *E. hibernica, E. erigena*) 'W. T. Rackcliff', cream-white – all these make a good display when there is little else in flower.

Summer and autumn flowering forms. Those worth considering include *Daboecia cantabrica* 'Alba', white; 'Atropurpurea', deep purple; and 'William Buchanan', crimson; *Calluna vulgaris* (syn. *Erica vulgaris*); 'County Wicklow', double pink; 'Golden Carpet', purple with leaves golden in summer and orange-red in winter; 'Multicolor', purple with leaves in shades of reds, yellows and oranges; 'Robert Chapman', similar but slightly taller; 'Silver Queen', purple with grey leaves; 'Sister Anne', pink with woolly grey leaves; 'Sunset', pink, with leaves turning from orange in spring to bronze in winter; 'White Lawn', white, light green foliage; 'Wickwar Flame', lavender, with orange-yellow summer foliage turning flame-red in winter; and 'Winter Chocolate', pale purple with green summer leaves turning to orange then chocolate in winter; also *Erica cinerea* 'Alba Minor', white; 'C. D. Eason', red-pink; 'Eden Valley', lavender and white flowers; 'Fiddler's Gold', lilac-pink with golden leaves; 'Purple Beauty'; 'Rock Pool', purple with gold leaves turning bronze in winter; 'Stephen Davis', magenta; and *Erica vagans* 'Lyonesse', white with bright green leaves; 'Mrs D. F. Maxwell', deep pink; 'Valerie Proudley', white with golden leaves; and 'St Keverne', salmon-pink.

Euonymus (spindle)

Hummock or sprawler. Evergreen. Although there is a number of deciduous forms of spindle, only the evergreen types of *Euonymus fortunei* (syn. *E. radicans*) make good ground coverers. These plants will thrive in almost any type of soil and grow well in sun or shade. Their flowers are inconspicuous but the foliage is frequently attractively variegated, making them particularly useful as foils for other plants, in borders, shrubberies, as low hedges or screens. Some useful forms include 'Colorata', green leaves turning purple in autumn, about 90 cm (3 ft) high by 2 m (6½ ft) spread; 'Emerald Cushion', emerald green foliage, 38 cm (15 in) in height and spread; 'Emerald Gaiety', slightly larger with silvery green leaves; 'Emerald 'n' Gold', again similar but with green, yellow-tinted leaves; 'Minima' (syn. 'Kewensis'), dark green leaves, very useful in the rock garden, growing only 10 cm (4 in) high with a spread of 45 cm (18 in); 'Silver Queen' (syn. 'Variegata'), young growth silvery turning to pink tints in autumn, 30 cm (1 ft) by 1.2 m (4 ft); 'Sunspot', dark green leaves with yellow mid-ribs, 30 cm (1 ft) by 45 cm (1½ ft); and 'Vegeta', glossy green leaves with orange berries in profusion in autumn, about 60 cm (2 ft) high by 2.5 m (8 ft) spread. Prune only if necessary. Propagate by division layering or by side-shoot cuttings in late summer.

Fuchsia

Hummock. Deciduous. Some hardy forms of fuchsias make good ground cover plants with their dense foliage and colourful display of pendulous flowers in late summer. They may be cut back to the ground by frosts but each spring will produce new growths from the base. To help overcome this problem, protecting the crowns in winter with peat, coarse sand, straw or cloches will be found useful. All will tolerate any soil, preferably reasonably moist, and they grow best in sunny positions. Useful varieties include 'Madame Cornelissen', about 60 cm (2 ft) by 1.2 m (4 ft) with dark green leaves and scarlet and white flowers; 'Mrs Popple', an arching variety 80 cm (2½ ft) by 80 cm (2½ ft) which has crimson and purple flowers; 'Riccartonii', 1.5 m (5 ft) by 1.5 m (5 ft), one of the hardiest fuchsias with scarlet and purple blooms; and 'Versicolor' (syn. 'Tricolor'), 80 cm (2½ ft) by 1 m (3¼ ft), copper-pink young leaves turning red and creamy later with crimson-purple flowers. Hard prune in spring. Propagate by tip cuttings in spring.

Gaultheria

Hummock or spreader. Evergreen. Although gaultherias must have lime-free soil, they are excellent ground coverers for large rock gardens, woodland areas, wild or peat gardens or mixed borders. They grow best in shade in soil which does not dry out. *Gaultheria cuneata* makes a neat hummock of shiny leaves with sprays of white bell-shaped flowers in summer followed by white berries in autumn. It grows to a height of about 30 cm (1 ft) and spreads about 1.2 m (4 ft). *G. procumbens* carpets the ground with shiny dark green leaves, summer white flowers and bright red berries in autumn. Its height is only about 8 cm (3 in) but it spreads 90 cm (3 ft) or more. For large gardens, the densely growing *G. shallon* is ideal under trees, growing over 2 m (7 ft) high and wide. Its leaves are broad and leathery and its pale pink flowers which appear in early summer are followed by purple-black berries. Pruning is not required. Propagate by division, layers or heel cuttings in summer, or by seed from ripe berries.

Genista (broom)

Hummock or carpeter. Deciduous. Like Cytisus (see p. 66), these brooms produce a mass of almost leafless stems, sometimes spiny, which form a sufficiently dense mass to be good ground coverers. Similarly they also grow well in well-drained soil and like plenty of sun. The low growing forms are suitable for borders, walls of rock gardens and all have yellow flowers in summer. Some useful ones from which to choose include *Genista hispanica*, about 60 cm (2 ft) by 90 cm (3 ft), stiff and spiny; *G. lydia*, about the same, but much quicker growing and with arching slender stems; *G. pilosa*, 30 cm (1 ft) by 60 cm (2 ft); *G. p.* 'Lemon Spreader', almost evergreen, 30 cm (1 ft) by 60 cm (2 ft); and *G. tinctoria* 'Plena', again of similar size but nearly leafless. Prune only if required. Propagate by stem cuttings in summer.

Hebe (veronica)

Hummock or carpeter. Evergreen. These plants grow well in all but the coldest parts of the country and are best given a sunny position in well-drained soil; protection of other taller plants from cold east and north winds is advisable. They grow freely in coastal regions and towns and their attractive foliage makes them useful year-round plants for rockeries, shrubberies, mixed borders and container growing. In recent years many new varieties have been introduced, and there is a wide range from which to choose. For ground cover, those with lance-shaped leaves serve the purpose better than the 'whipcord' (conifer-like) types. Some suitable forms include *Hebe albicans*, white summer flowers, grey leaves, 30 cm (1 ft) high by 60 cm (2 ft) spread; *H.* 'Carl Teschner', purple summer flowers, dark green leaves, of similar height and spread; *H. colensoi*, white summer flowers, waxy grey leaves, height and spread about 60 cm (2 ft); *H. pinguifolia* 'Pagei', white flowers in early summer, blue-grey leaves, 23 cm (9 in) by 45 cm (1½ ft); and *H. subalpina* (syn. *H. rakaiensis*), white summer flowers, light bright green foliage, about 60 cm (2 ft) by 60 cm (2 ft). Prune in spring if necessary to keep growth compact, and remove dead flower heads. Propagate by stem cuttings in summer or division of the carpeters in autumn.

Hedera (ivy) (See Chapter 10)

Helianthemum (rock rose, sun rose)
Hummock. Evergreen. Rock roses make excellent ground coverers in rock gardens, over walls and banks, and as edges to borders. Their brightly coloured flowers throughout summer make a mass of brilliance, and the green or grey leaves are a welcome attraction at any time of year. All like a well-drained soil and a sunny position. Most commonly grown are those called the 'Garden Hybrids', which reach a height of 30 cm (1 ft) and spread 60 cm (2 ft) or more. Among good named forms are 'Amy Baring', orange; 'Fireball' (syn. 'Mrs Earle'), red, double flowers; 'Jubilee', double yellow; 'Mrs Moules', orange-pink; 'Praecox', yellow; 'Rhodanthe Carneum', pink, grey leaves; 'Wisley Pink', pink, grey leaves; 'Wisley White', white, grey leaves; and 'Wisley Primrose',

Fig. 9 *Hypericum* (St John's wort, rose of Sharon). Evergreen; has yellow cup-shaped flowers throughout summer. Its quickly spreading habit is useful in awkward north-facing beds where little else will grow.

yellow, grey leaves. Prune with shears after flowering to encourage fresh new growth to maintain good ground cover. Propagate by heel side-shoot cuttings in summer.

Hypericum (St John's wort, rose of Sharon) (Fig. 9)

Hummock or spreader. Evergreen or semi-evergreen. The most popular St John's wort, which grows freely in any well-drained soil in sun or shade and which forms a good ground coverer, is *Hypericum calycinum*. With its evergreen leaves, which take on a purple tinge in autumn, yellow cup-shaped flowers throughout summer, and its spreading habit, it quickly forms a dense mass which looks attractive in shrubberies, wild gardens or in awkward north-facing beds where little else will grow. It grows about 30 cm (1 ft) high but spreads indefinitely. *H.* × *moserianum* is not dissimilar but grows about 60 cm (2 ft) high and spreads about 90 cm (3 ft). Its variety 'Tricolor' is smaller, not always fully hardy, but has handsome green and yellow, red-edged foliage; it grows freely in a sunny position. Pruning of *H. calycinum* each spring, by cutting back the stems to within a few inches of the base, is recommended but not essential to keep the plants dense. The other forms should require little or no pruning. Propagate *H. calycinum* by division between autumn and spring and other forms by side-shoot cuttings in early summer.

Juniperus (juniper) (Fig. 10)

Hummock or carpeter. Evergreen. Of conifers, the *Juniperus* genus offers by far the largest selection of medium height, low-growing or prostrate shrubs for ground cover. Most are excellent for rock gardens, banks, mixed borders, among heathers and heaths, in wild gardens, in containers, or for hiding ground level eyesores such as manhole covers. They are hardy, will grow well in either acid or alkaline soil, prefer sun but will tolerate light shade, and are excellent at smothering weeds. The foliage may be what is called 'juvenile' (awl-shaped, the overall effect being feathery) or 'adult' (scale-like and pressed closely to the stem), and sometimes both types are found on the same plant. The colour of the foliage varies among the forms, making them particularly attractive all year round. Of the many forms from which to choose are: *Juniperus communis* 'Depressa Aurea', golden in summer, bronze in winter, about 15 cm (6 in) high by 1.5 m (5 ft) spread; *J. c.* 'Repanda', dark green, similar height and spread; *J. conferta*, bluish green, 15 cm (6 in) by 1.5 m (5 ft); *J. c.* 'Expansa Variegata', yellowy-white variegated foliage, 15 cm (6 in) by 90 cm (3 ft); *J. horizontalis* 'Bar Harbor', grey-green, 15 cm (6 in) by up to 2 m (6½ ft); *J. h.* 'Blue Moon' (syn. 'Blue Chip'), silver-blue in summer, blue-grey in winter, 15 cm (6 in) by 90 cm (3 ft); *J. h.* 'Douglasii', blue-green in summer, purplish in winter, 15 cm (6 in) by

Fig. 10 *Juniperus communis* 'Depressa Aurea' (juniper). Evergreen, excellent for rock gardens; foliage is golden in summer, bronze in winter, about 15 cm (6 in) high by 1.5 m (5 ft) spread.

up to 2 m (6½ ft); *J. h.* 'Emerald Spreader', emerald green, 10 cm (4 in) by 2 m (6½ ft); *J. h.* 'Glauca', steel blue, 15 cm (6 in) by 1.5 m (5 ft); *J. h.* 'Plumosa Youngstown', bright green in summer, bronze in winter, up to 30 cm (1 ft) by 1.2 m (4 ft); *J. × media* 'Old Gold', golden, 90 cm (3 ft) by 1.5 m (5 ft); *J. procumbens* 'Nana', apple green, 30 cm (1 ft) by 1.5 m (5 ft); *J. sabina* 'Hicksii', grey-blue, 60 cm (2 ft) by 90 cm (3 ft); *J. s.* 'Scandia' (syn. 'Scandens'), dark green, 30 cm (1 ft) by 90 cm (3 ft); *J. s.* 'Variegata', variegated green and white, 30 cm (1 ft) by 90 cm (3 ft); *J. s.* 'Tamariscifolia', dark blue-green, similar height and spread; *J. s.* 'Sargentii', apple green, prickly, 30 cm (1 ft) by up to 1.5 m (5 ft); *J. squamata* 'Blue Carpet', silver-blue, about 20 cm (8 in) by up to 2 m (6½ ft); *J. virginiana* 'Blue Cloud', silver-grey, somewhat twisted branches, 45 cm (1½ ft) by up to 1.5 m (5 ft); and *J. v.* 'Grey Owl', faster-growing, silvery grey, 60 cm (2 ft) by up to 3 m (10 ft). Pruning the shoots in late spring helps to maintain a bushy dense growth. Propagate by side-shoot cuttings in autumn.

Lavandula (lavender)

Hummock. Evergreen. All lavenders make reasonably good ground coverers but, as they tend to grow leggy and thin after five or six years, they generally need replacing if they are to be effective. All do well in light soil and sun and their purple, lavender-pink or white spikes of sweet-scented flowers in summer and aromatic grey-green leaves make them popular garden plants for low hedges or in borders. The best form to grow as ground cover is the Dutch Lavender, *Lavandula spica* 'Vera', which has a height of about 60 cm (2 ft) and spread of 90 cm (3 ft); its smaller, more compact form, *L. s.* 'Nana Alba', with white flowers is also effective. The Old English Lavenders, *L. s.* 'Hidcote' and *L. s.* 'Munstead', with purple flowers, both grow to a height and spread of about 60 cm (2 ft) and form reasonably compact bushes. Prune every spring by clipping the plants with shears to keep them producing new bushy growth. Propagate by heel cuttings in late summer.

Lonicera (honeysuckle) (See also Chapter 10)
Hummock. Evergreen. Bush honeysuckles have the advantage over their climbing forms in that they grow well in almost any soil and in sun or shade. They are useful for growing in wild or woodland gardens, in shrubberies or for making low hedges. The best ground covering form is *Lonicera pileata* which has bright green leaves, inconspicuous flowers and semi-transparent purplish fruits in late summer; its ultimate height is about 90 cm (3 ft) with a spread up to 1.5 m (5 ft). *L. nitida* 'Baggesen's Gold', with its yellow leaves, is also effective, with a height and spread of about 1.5 m (5 ft); it prefers full sun. Prune to maintain shape. Propagate by layering or stem cuttings in summer.

Leucothoe
Spreader. Evergreen. Of this genus only *Leucothoe fontanesiana* 'Rainbow' is really suitable as a ground coverer but its attractive yellow, pink and cream variegated leaves make it particularly effective for growing in acid soils in a lightly shaded position. It produces bunches of small white flowers in early summer and grows to a height and spread of about 1.5 m (5 ft). Prune after flowering to encourage density. Propagate by stem cuttings or layering in summer.

Mahonia (Oregon grape)
Spreader. Evergreen. Of this genus, only one really makes a good ground coverer and that is *Mahonia aquifolium*. It makes excellent cover in woodlands or places where it is in shade, though it does equally well in sun. It tolerates most soils, but fails to spread effectively if too dry. Its shiny dark green divided leaves make a very good contrast to many other evergreens, and they have the added benefit of sometimes turning purple and red in winter. The clusters of golden yellow fragrant flowers in spring are followed by blue-black berries. It grows about 60 cm (2 ft) high and spreads up to 1.5 m (5 ft). Its form 'Atropurpurea' is similar, with red to purple leaves in winter and spring. It is sometimes slow growing but once established is very effective. Pruning is usually unnecessary but cutting it down in spring helps to keep the plant low growing. Propagate by

Potentilla 'Red Ace' (cinquefoil) forms an attractive and dense small bush.

division or layers in autumn or spring, seeds sown in summer or stem cuttings in early summer.

Pachysandra (Japanese spurge)

Carpeter. Evergreen. *Pachysandra terminalis* is one of the best ground coverers, its rich green leaves, usually in whorls, forming a dense carpeting effect. Its white spring flowers are fairly inconspicuous. Because it grows well in any soil, and does not object to dry shady positions, it is particularly useful in narrow north-facing borders, in woodland or in shrubberies. Height and spread are about 23 cm (9 in) by 45 cm (18 in). *P. t.* 'Variegata' is similar but with variegated white leaves. Pruning is unnecessary. Propagate by division in spring.

Pernettya

Spreader. Evergreen. Pernettyas are particularly striking glossy-leaved evergreens which must be grown in an acid soil, but are tolerant of sun or light shade, and which produce white bell-shaped heather-like flowers in early summer followed by shiny long-lasting berries, provided at least one male form is planted to every three female forms. *P. mucronata* is most commonly grown and the berries vary in colour according to which form is planted, e.g. 'Bell's Seedling' fruits are large and bright red; 'Crimsoniana', crimson; 'Cherry Ripe', cherry red; 'Lilian', pink; and 'Snow White'. Bushes grow to a height and spread of about 60 cm (2 ft). A mixed group in a shrub border or a light woodland can look very effective. Prune in late winter or early spring if the plants tend to get straggly. Propagate by division or heel cuttings in autumn.

Potentilla (cinquefoil)

Hummock. Deciduous. Of the shrubby cinquefoils, *Potentilla fruticosa* and its varieties are by far the most popular and efficient as ground covers. (See Chapter 8 for the herbaceous forms.) They all form thick-set dense little bushes and are excellent for the front of mixed or shrub borders. They bear their green or greyish foliage for much of the year, and in most cases the strawberry-like flowers are yellow or white and are borne from early summer until autumn. Some good forms from which to choose include: 'Abbotswood', white flowers, grey-green leaves, 80 cm (2½ ft) high by up to 1.5 m (5 ft) spread; 'Elizabeth', yellow flowers, green leaves, 60 cm (2 ft) by 1.5 m (5 ft); 'Farreri', deep, bright yellow flowers, fern-like green leaves, 1.2 m (4 ft) by 1.2 m (4 ft); 'Katherine Dykes', paler yellow; 'Longacre', pale yellow, greyish green foliage, 60 cm (2 ft) by 1.2 m (4 ft); 'Mandschurica', white, silver-grey leaves, 30 cm (1 ft) by 90 cm (3 ft); 'Primrose Beauty', cream, greyish green leaves, 80 cm (2½ ft) by 1.2 m (4 ft); 'Red Ace', unique colour form of mainly bright red flowers and green leaves, 60 cm (2 ft) by

1.2 m (4 ft); and 'Tangerine', light orange and bright green foliage, 45 cm (1½ ft) by 90 cm (3 ft). Prune hard in spring if the plants get too tall or become straggly. Propagate by layering or side-shoot cuttings in autumn.

Prunus (cherry laurel)

Hummock. Evergreen. Cherry laurels are valuable shrubs in that they thrive in almost any soil (except a poorly drained one) and like sun or shade. They are ideal for woodland or wild areas or as taller specimen ground cover shrubs in a border. They have handsome glossy green leaves and bear white or pale yellow flowers in early summer. *Prunus laurocerasus* 'Otto Luyken' is the most popular form, reaching a height of 1.2 m (4 ft) and a spread of 1.5 m (5 ft). 'Schipkaensis' and 'Zabeliana', similar but slightly larger, are equally good ground coverers. Prune in spring to remove dead wood and maintain shape if necessary. Propagate by side-shoot heel cuttings in late summer.

Rhododendron (rhododendron, azalea)

Hummock. Evergreen. There are several thousands of rhododendron and azalea (which are rhododendrons) species, hybrids and varieties, a great number of which are suitable for use as ground coverers. These ground coverers vary in height from being almost prostrate to making large bushes 2 m (6 ft) in height and spread. One thing they all have in common is that they must be grown in an acid soil, which preferably contains a high humus content. Like ericas, they can be grown in peat beds and given a Sequestrene compound annually. They also tend to prefer light shade rather than deep woodland or open, very sunny situations. Because of the range of sizes, light woodland, shrubberies, rockeries or containers can all accommodate rhododendrons. Their evergreen leaf form is usually lance shaped and may be large or small, of various shades of green, or even grey, bronze, or blue in colour, and sometimes with coloured 'felted' undersurface. In the case of azaleas the leaves often turn red, yellow and purple in autumn. The funnel shaped trusses of flowers are produced in late spring or early or mid-summer in a vast range of colours, either a single colour, multicoloured or blotched. It is not possible to list all the many forms suitable for ground covering as so much depends on the situation in which the rhododendron is to be grown and personal preference as to the habit, leaf and flower colour. It is advisable, however, to select only the evergreen forms of azaleas and to make certain the plants are fully hardy. Pruning is usually unnecessary but it is important to remove the dead flower heads. Propagate by layering at any time of year (but best in spring) or by heel cuttings in mid-summer.

A collection of rhododendrons at the RHS Gardens, Wisley, gives evergreen coverage and spring flowers.

Ribes (flowering currant)
Hummock. Deciduous. Only one species, *Ribes alpinum*, makes a good ground covering plant from this genus. It will grow in any soil, in sun or shade, and is useful for hedging or in shrub borders and light woodland. It has green-lobed leaves, which often colour in autumn, and bears erect spikes of greenish flowers in spring followed by red berries. It grows to a height and spread of about 1.2 m (4 ft). Prune hard after flowering to remove dead wood from ground level. Propagate by stem cuttings in early winter or layering in spring or autumn.

Rosa (rose) (See also Chapter 10)
Hummock or carpeter. Deciduous. Only shrub roses suitable as ground coverers are included in this chapter; other lax-growing rambling forms are described in Chapter 10. Although there are many hundreds of types, species, varieties and hybrids of roses, only very few of the shrub types make efficient ground coverers; even then, they will probably require weeding for the first year or two until they are established and have formed a dense cover. All roses like a medium type of soil, preferably enriched with humus, and they flower best in full sun. The forms mentioned are excellent for shrub borders, wild gardens, patios (the smaller

Santolina neapolitana (cotton lavender) makes a lovely colour combination of grey foliage and yellow flowers.

types), containers, growing over walls, banks or eyesores at ground level and for growing in beds on their own. For large gardens 'Max Graf' is an almost evergreen carpeter about 90 cm (3 ft) high spreading up to 2.5 m (8¼ ft) which has small glossy leaves and clusters of bright pink flowers for a long period in late summer. *Rosa wichuraiana* is somewhat similar in size and habit, is almost evergreen and has clusters of small white flowers; also similar but very thorny are R. × *paulii*, white flowers, and R. × *paulii* 'Rosea', pink flowers. For smaller gardens 'Fru Dagmar Hastrup' (syn. 'Frau Dagmar Hartopp') makes a bush about 1.2 m (4 ft) in height and spread, has dark crinkled foliage and continuous summer clusters of single pink flowers followed by red hips. 'Nozomi' is more dainty, growing about 60 cm (2 ft) by 90 cm (3 ft), with large trusses of pale pink flowers. *R. nitida* is a dwarf twiggy form about 60 cm (2 ft) by 60 cm (2 ft), small glossy leaves that turn scarlet in autumn, and bright pink flowers followed by red hips; 'The Fairy' is a vigorous, spreading rose, 60 cm (2 ft) by 1.2 m (4 ft), with rose-pink blooms produced freely and small abundant leaves. Among some of the newer roses, which are now officially classified as ground cover roses, are 'Grouse', pale pink, single; 'Pheasant', light pink, double; 'Partridge', white, single, all of which grow about 30 cm (1 ft) high by 1.5 m (5 ft) spread; 'Snow Carpet', white, double, 15 cm (6 in) by 75 cm (2½ ft); 'Red Blanket', red, single; 'Rosy Cushion', pink, white-eyed single; and 'Smarty', pale pink, single. These last three grow about 50 cm (20 in) high and spread 90 cm (3 ft). These newer types of ground cover roses are repeat flowering and their dense, glossy foliage tends to be retained by the plants for some ten months of the year. Prune only to remove dead wood and keep the roses in good shape. Propagate by non-flowering side-shoot cuttings in late summer.

Rosmarinus (rosemary)

Sprawler or hummock. Evergreen. The hardy form commonly available for ground cover purposes is *Rosmarinus officinalis*, which forms a loose-growing dense shrub suitable for walls, banks and informal hedges. It grows freely in full sun and well-drained soil and can reach a height and spread of up to 2 m (6½ ft). It is always a popular shrub with its all-year-round aromatic small grey-green leaves and clusters of pale lavender flowers in late spring. Prune after flowering to keep the bush tidy. R. o. 'McConnells Blue' is a relatively vigorous prostrate form which makes an attractive spreading hummock covered with blue flowers in late spring and early summer. It grows about 40 cm (16 in) tall with a 1 m (3¼ ft) spread. Propagate by stem cuttings in late summer or by layering in autumn or spring.

Rubus (ornamental bramble)
Carpeter. Evergreen. Of the ornamental bramble, two species make good ground coverers. Both will grow in any soil, provided it is not poorly drained, and thrive in sun or dense shade. The smallest is *Rubus calycinoides* (syn. *R. fockeanus*), growing about 8 cm (3 in) high and spreading 60 cm (24 in), so making it useful for rockeries, walls or in shrubberies. It forms dense carpets of rooting stems covered with glossy green lobed leaves with a white undersurface. The white summer flowers are inconspicuous. Another species, *R. tricolor*, is one of the most useful ground coverers, particularly for bigger gardens where it looks highly effective under trees. It grows about 15 cm (6 in) high and spreads 3.5 m (11 ft) or more. Its glossy green leaves with white undersurfaces cover bristly rooting stems and its white flowers in summer are sometimes followed by edible red fruits. It may need weeding the first year or two until established. Pruning is usually unnecessary. Propagate *R. calycinoides* by division in autumn or spring, *R. tricolor* by natural tip layers or stem cuttings in autumn.

Salvia (sage)
Hummock. Evergreen. *Salvia officinalis* and its forms most commonly grown as ground coverers are sometimes listed under herbs rather than shrubs as they are widely used in cooking. They do, however, make very useful edgings for borders, on patios or in containers. They prefer light soil in a sunny position, preferably with some protection from cold winter winds and frosts as they can be cut back by hard weather, though will recover quickly in the spring. *Salvia officinalis* has grey-green woolly leaves, lavender flowers in mid-summer and grows about 60 cm (2 ft) in height and spread. Its two forms 'Icterina', with grey-green leaves variegated yellow, and 'Purpurescens', with purplish foliage, are similar in habit but slightly less hardy. Prune regularly by trimming to keep the plants dense. Propagate by division, layering or stem cuttings in autumn or seed sown in spring.

Santolina (cotton lavender)
Hummock. Evergreen. Cotton lavenders make a delightful silvery-leaved foil for many other garden plants and grow well in sunny positions in well-drained soil at the front of shrubberies, in mixed borders, rock gardens or as dwarf hedges. *Santolina chamaecyparissus* (syn. *S. incana*), growing 45 cm (1½ ft) high by 60 cm (2 ft), has fragrant woolly grey leaves and clusters of yellow flowers in summer. Its form *S. c.* 'Nana' is about half the size but similar in appearance. *S. neapolitana*, with a height and spread of about 90 cm (3 ft), is looser in growth than the other two and has more feathery fragrant foliage. Prune in spring or after

flowering by clipping with shears to remove sufficient top growth to encourage the plants to throw new shoots from the base and so remain dense and bushy. Propagate by division in spring or by late summer stem cuttings.

Sarcococca

Hummock. Evergreen. Very useful ground coverers for shady places in shrubberies or under trees. They like a fairly rich soil and are best grouped together for full effect. Their shining dark leaves are striking all year round and their somewhat inconspicuous tassels of whitish fragrant flowers in winter are followed by black or red fruits. The two forms commonly available are *Sarcococca humilis* and *S. hookeriana digyna*; the former grows 45 cm (1½ ft) tall and spreads 75 cm (2½ ft), while the latter is about 60 cm (2 ft) tall with a spread of up to 1.8 m (6 ft). Prune to remove old shoots after flowering. Propagate by division of their spreading roots in spring or stem cuttings in autumn.

Senecio greyi (syn. *S.* × Dunedin Hybrid 'Sunshine'), the best of the silver foliage ground cover plants.

A selection of ground cover plants showing *Viburnum davidii* in the centre with its veined leaves and white flowers.

Senecio

Hummock. Evergreen. Although *Senecio laxifolius* and *S. greyi* are listed as available species in most catalogues, these garden plants are now both known to be a hybrid and their correct name is *S.* × Dunedin Hybrids 'Sunshine'. It is sufficiently hardy to be grown anywhere in well-drained soil and a sunny position in the garden. It is, however, probably the best of silver foliage shrubs and particularly useful for contrasting with green-leaved plants, especially for winter effect. It looks equally effective in gardens of all sizes. Not only are the oval leaves truly grey on the upper surface, but virtually white underneath; they are carried on white shoots when young. The yellow daisy-like flowers are borne in mid-summer, followed by feathery seed heads which are best removed. Its average height is about 90 cm (3 ft) but spread up to 1.5 m (5 ft). Prune by clipping in spring (which prevents flowering but encourages bushiness) or cut back old shoots after flowering. Propagate by stem cuttings in late summer or layering in autumn.

Skimmia

Hummock. Evergreen. Skimmias grow well in any fertile soil, preferably not chalky, and are best grown in shade. They are taller than many ground cover plants and particularly useful in shrubberies, light woodland or wild gardens. Their ultimate height is about 1.2 m (4 ft) and spread up to 1.8 m (6 ft). They have aromatic glossy green leaves and sweetly scented spikes of white or ivory, sometimes red-budded, flowers in spring. These are followed by long-lasting red berries in late summer, provided at least one male form is planted with three female forms. Most commonly grown is *Skimmia japonica* (female), and the male form 'Rubella', which bears red flower buds through the winter before opening a creamy colour. Pruning is unnecessary. Propagate by stem cuttings in summer or by layering in autumn.

Taxus (yew)

Hummock. Evergreen. *Taxus baccata*, the common yew, is widely grown as a specimen tree or for hedging, but its less well known form, *T. b.* 'Repandens', makes an excellent ground cover plant. It tolerates almost any position and soil and its deep green leaves on pendulous branches make it an attractive sight. It grows about 45 cm (1½ ft) high and will spread 1.5 m (5 ft) quite easily. Like other conifers, it is excellent for covering retaining walls or ground level eyesores, such as manhole covers. A new form, *T. b.* 'Repens Aurea', is somewhat taller and less spreading but its golden yellow foliage can offer a good contrast to other plants. No pruning is necessary. Propagate by stem cuttings in autumn, or layering in spring or autumn.

Tsuga (hemlock)
Hummock. Evergreen. Although hemlocks are usually tall-growing conifers there are some dwarf and slow-growing forms of *Tsuga canadensis* which have drooping branches and make good dense ground coverers. All grow well in any soil in sunny or lightly shaded positions. They are excellent in heather borders, or on walls, banks or in larger rockeries where they can drape themselves downwards. *T. c.* 'Bennett' has mid-green leaves, *T. c.* 'Jeddeloh', light green foliage, *T. c.* 'Nana Gracilis', similar but with light green leaves, and *T. c.* 'Pendula', the most drooping with pale green foliage; all grow about 30 cm (1 ft) high and spread 60–90 cm (2–3 ft) over a ten- or twelve-year period. Ultimately *T. c.* 'Pendula' can reach as much as 2 m (6½ ft) high and spread 4 m (13 ft). Prune as required to keep them in shape. Propagate by stem cuttings in autumn.

Vaccinium (cowberry, mountain cranberry)
Spreader. Evergreen. Only one form is generally available as a good ground coverer and that is *Vaccinium vitis-idaea*, usually in the form 'Koralle'. It likes a rich acid soil and is tolerant of shade, making it useful in peat borders or light woodland areas. It has a creeping habit, small oval evergreen leaves which are tinted bronze in winter, and pink bell-shaped flowers in summer followed by edible red fruits. It grows about 15 cm (6 in) high and spreads up to 45 cm (1½ ft). Prune by clipping over in spring to keep it bushy. Propagate by layering or division in autumn.

Viburnum
Hummock. Evergreen. *Viburnum davidii* is the most suitable species in this genus for ground covering. It grows 60–90 cm (2–3 ft) high, spreads 1.2–1.5 m (4–5 ft), and does best in any reasonably good soil in either sun or shade. It is suitable for shrubberies, mixed borders, light woodland or in containers. It has dark deeply-veined large leaves of glossy green, flat heads of white flowers in early summer and, provided a male and female form are planted alongside each other, the female produces clusters of pretty turquoise-blue berries. Prune only to remove dead wood and keep to shape in spring. Propagate by layering or stem cuttings in autumn.

Vinca (periwinkle)
Carpeter. Evergreen. All periwinkles make excellent ground coverers, growing in any soil, in sun or shade. They spread freely by their rooting trailing stems and are useful for woodlands, banks, wild gardens, shady borders, by buildings, or as 'carpets' in shrubberies. *Vinca major* and *V. minor* are the two most popular species grown and both have a number of

varieties. *V. major* grows about 45 cm (1½ ft) tall and spreads 90–120 cm (3–4 ft) and *V. minor*, more suitable for smaller gardens, is about 15 cm (6 in) high and spreads 60–90 cm (2–3 ft). The species have shiny pointed green leaves and lavender-blue flowers in spring. Some of their varieties have variegated leaves, while others produce purple, white or blue flowers. All may require hand weeding for the first year or so until established. Pruning is generally unnecessary, except to trim with shears in spring to keep to shape. Propagate by division any time between autumn and spring.

CHAPTER 10

CLIMBERS AND RAMBLERS

It may seem somewhat unusual to include climbing and rambling plants in a book about ground coverers, but the genera mentioned in this chapter are all extremely useful for this purpose, especially in largish gardens. Most grow fairly quickly but it is advisable to plant them in clean ground initially and then weed for the first year or two if necessary.

Unless the objective is to allow these plants to ramble over unsightly tree stumps or other unwanted plants, they should not be planted close to trees or shrubs or they will quickly start scrambling over and tend to smother them. Their ideal places are banks, walls, wild gardens, to cover unsightly areas of concrete or paving, or to give interest to level areas which would otherwise be dull and colourless.

Holding some of the stems down with bricks, stones or wooden pegs will help them to root into a ground covering position and become effective weed smotherers. Once established they require very little attention and can give areas of interest for all or much of the year.

The plants described are mainly creepers and twiners and some sprawlers, and the definition of these terms is given on p. 9. As with all the other plants referred to in this book, only average heights and spreads can be given, as ultimate size will depend on the situation in which they are grown. All the plants named here are hardy, and brief mention of any pruning necessary and methods of propagation are given.

Clematis (Fig. 11)
Creeper. Deciduous or evergreen. Clematis species can make extremely effective ground coverers where they have the space necessary to spread. They grow best if their roots are planted in a shady cool position with the foliage and flowers in sun and they will tolerate any soil but, in general, prefer an alkaline one. They are excellent for banks, walls or in wild gardens, but, as their twining leaf stalks help them to scramble over plants or other obstacles in their path, it is often advisable to hold the shoots down with wooden pegs or bricks. The two evergreen species are *Clematis armandii*, which can be kept to a height of about 30 cm (12 in) but will spread up to 11 m (36 ft) or more, which has shiny dark green leaves, and clusters of ivory-white flowers in spring, and *C. calycina* (syn.

Fig. 11 Clematis species can make effective ground coverers providing they have the space to spread. Will grow best if roots are planted in shady, cool position and with foliage and flowers in the sun.

C. balearica), which grows to a height of about 30 cm (12 in), spreads about 2.4 m (8 ft), and has green fern-like foliage which turns bronze in winter and enhances the pale yellow flowers produced in late winter. With the deciduous species, all can be kept to a height of about 30 cm (12 in) with a spread of 1.5 m (5 ft) to 12 m (40 ft), or less if the plants are cut back. *C. flammula* has small green leaves and fragrant white late summer flowers in clusters which are followed by fluffy seed heads. *C. montana*, early summer white flowers and *C. m.* 'Rubens', rosy red blooms and early purple-tinged leaves, are both attractive, and the autumn flowering *C. orientalis* with yellow flower bells followed by silvery seed heads has grey-green leaves, and *C. tangutica*, similar but with green leaves, give late season interest. Prune back unwanted growths of all forms in early spring. Propagate by layering in early spring or stem cuttings in summer.

Hedera (ivy)

Carpeter. Evergreen. Ivies make superb ground covering plants, growing virtually prostrate but often spreading more than 2 m (6½ ft) and providing a wealth of different coloured toothed, lobed or heart-shaped leaf forms. They will grow well in any soil, except very dry or very wet, and are equally happy in sun or shade. They look very effective when grown under trees, in shrubberies, down banks or walls or in patio soil pockets, when they will form dense weed-suppressing carpets. The species most suitable are *Hedera canariensis*, *H. colchica* and *H. helix*, but all three are represented by numerous variegated leaf forms which may be yellow, silver or white. For example, *H. canariensis* 'Variegata' has olive-green leaves with silver and white margins often turning bronzish in winter; *H. colchica dentata* 'Aurea' has soft green and yellow variegated foliage; *H. c.* 'Paddy's Pride' has leaves with an irregular central yellow splash of colour; *H. helix* 'Marginata' (syn. 'Argentea Elegans') has greyish green leaves with creamy- or pink-tinged margins while *H. h.* 'Buttercup' has golden leaves and *H. h.* 'Gold Heart', a central yellow blotch. There are very many others available from which to choose, but make sure you select the hardy outdoor forms and not those most suited to indoor pot culture. Yellow-green flowers followed by black berries are occasionally produced in autumn on ivies used as ground cover. Prune only if necessary in early spring. Propagate by layering any time or stem cuttings in summer or autumn.

Hydrangea

Carpeter. Deciduous. Only one species, *Hydrangea petiolaris*, is really suitable for ground cover. It will grow well in any soil, but produces in summer some creamy white flower clusters most freely in a sunny position. It produces self-clinging roots on its shoots and these will root if pegged down to the soil. Pegging down will also help the large green leaves form a good cover. Height and spread are about 60 cm (2 ft) by 1.5 m (5 ft). It looks particularly effective on banks and walls or over tree stumps in wild gardens. Pruning is usually unnecessary. Propagate by layering at any time or by stem cuttings in summer.

Lathyrus (everlasting pea) (See also Chapter 7)

Creeper. Deciduous. Allowed to ramble at will over dry slopes or in a wild garden, the hardy everlasting pea with its deep pink, pale pink and white pea-like flowers produced over a long period and greyish green leaves makes an attractive sight and is a good ground coverer. *Lathyrus latifolius* is most commonly grown and, unlike annual sweet peas (see *Lathyrus*, Chapter 7) it is a perennial. Allowed to ramble, it will grow about 60 cm (2 ft) high and about 2 m (6½ ft) wide. Prune current year's growths back to 30 cm (1 ft) in early winter. Propagate by seed in spring or division in early spring.

Lonicera (honeysuckle) (See also Chapter 9)

Twiner. Evergreen or deciduous. Left to their own devices without supports up which to grow, honeysuckles form a good bushy type of ground cover, especially the evergreen forms. They grow best in a rich moist soil but tolerate sun or shade and are excellent for banks, walls or light woodland areas. Holding down some of the stems with pegs or stones helps to keep the plants dense and encourages rooting. Height and spread of the forms usually grown for this purpose and in this way are about 30 cm (1 ft) by 1.5 m (5 ft). *Lonicera japonica* is the best evergreen species and is usually available in the forms 'Aureo-reticulata', small leaves netted with yellow veins and scented yellow flowers in summer; 'Halliana', pale green leaves and whitish fragrant flowers from mid-summer until mid-autumn; and *L. j. repens* (syn. *flexuosa*), which has purplish young shoots and leaves and reddish flower buds opening to white fragrant blooms from summer to mid-autumn. The two deciduous twining honeysuckles which are most popular are *L. periclymenum* 'Belgica', the early Dutch honeysuckle (which is often the common *L. caprifolium* 'Pauciflora') with purple, red and yellow flowers in early summer, and *L. p.* 'Serotina', the late Dutch honeysuckle, with rather deeper coloured flowers from mid-summer to autumn. Both have dark green leaves and, planted together, give a long season of colour and fragrance. Prune by clipping back in spring if the plants get untidy. Propagate by layering in late summer or stem cuttings in summer.

Parthenocissus (syn. *Ampelopsis*) (Virginia creeper)
Creeper. Deciduous. Virginia creepers are grown mainly for their mat of dark green, large, lobed leaves, that produce a wonderful mass of different red shades in autumn. The flowers are inconspicuous. They grow happily in any reasonably well-drained soil, in sun or shade, and allowed to wander at will in a wild garden or over banks and walls they form effective cover for much of the year. Again, placing stones or pegs on the lower stems will encourage dense growth and stem rooting. Three good forms to choose include *Parthenocissus henryana*, with silver- and pink-veined leaves, *P. quinquefolia* (syn. *Vitis hederacea*), and *P. tricuspidata* (syn. *Ampelopsis veitchii*); all grow about 30 cm (1 ft) tall and will spread 3.6 cm (12 ft) or more. Pruning is usually unnecessary. Propagate by layering or stem cuttings in early winter.

Rosa (rose) (See also Chapter 9)
Sprawler. Deciduous or semi-evergreen. Some of the lax-growing rambler roses lend themselves ideally to growing as ground cover plants. They will grow well in any reasonably fertile soil but prefer a sunny position to flower freely, and an open position on banks or walls, or in wild gardens, will suit them admirably. Before planting the ground should be free of weeds, and hand weeding may be necessary for the first one or two years. It is also advisable to peg down some of the stems so that good ground cover is achieved. Of the varieties mentioned, all keep their leaves for a long period of the year — nine to ten months — and they

Clematis tangutica grows as well over the ground (for suppressing weeds) as it does as a climber.

flower freely in summer. The average height when allowed to ramble naturally is about 90 cm (3 ft) and spread is about 3 m (10 ft). Suitable varieties for the purpose include: 'Alberic Barbier', yellow buds turning white; 'Crimson Shower', crimson; 'Dorothy Perkins', rose pink; 'Excelsa', rosy crimson; 'François Juranville', fawn-pink; 'Sanders White', white; 'Temple Bells', white; and 'Veilchenblau', violet-blue. Prune only when necessary by cutting out old unwanted stems after flowering. Propagate by layering or non-flowering side-shoot cuttings in autumn.

Vitis (grape vine)

Creeper. Deciduous. The most suitable form for ground cover is *Vitis coignetiae* which, like *Parthenocissus*, spreads its creeping stems and large rounded leaves quickly to form effective cover for much of the year. Its main season of brilliance is in the autumn when the leaves turn yellow, orange and red. Its summer flowers are insignificant but fragrant, and the purplish black berries which follow are inedible. But a sheet of this grape vine spreading over a bank or in a wild garden, where the soil is fertile and it gets plenty of sun, is a lovely sight. Its height is about 30 cm (1 ft) and it spreads 3.6 m (12 ft) or more. Holding down some of the stems with pegs or stones will help establish cover and rooting. Prune only if required to keep to size. Propagate by layering in autumn.

CHAPTER 11

ORNAMENTAL GRASSES AND HARDY FERNS

Both these groups of plants have become more popular after a decline in the use of them in the past. Between them they offer a range of different leaf forms, often variegated or a colour other than green, which act as attractive foils to other types of broad leaved plants. Also, they will often grow well in areas where other plants will not give of their best.

In the case of grasses, although there are some attractive deciduous forms, as labour-saving coverers the evergreen ones are best used. Although the leaves are usually typically grass-like – thin and narrow – the density of them gives the desired effect. As a bonus, they produce flower heads which can either be left to seed or be used for flower arrangements. They are all easily propagated by division.

On the other hand, most ferns tend to be deciduous, and have no flowers, but their attractive leaf shapes, and the fact that the dead leaves can be left throughout winter to continue serving the purpose of ground cover makes them an attractive addition to any garden. On the whole, it is generally best to purchase evergreen ferns if possible. Again, all can be propagated by division.

Both grasses and ferns are either clump formers or spreaders, see pp. 8–9 for description, and the heights and spreads given are average for most conditions.

Ornamental grasses

Carex morrowii 'Evergold' (of gardens) has attractive arching yellow and green leaves which remain colourful all year round. It will grow easily in any situation and reaches a height of about 20 cm (8 in) and spreads about 45 cm (1½ ft). It looks elegant in any type of border or as a specimen plant in a container.

Festuca glauca forms a dense mass of blue-grey leaves and reaches a height and spread of about 15 cm (6 in) by 25 cm (10 in). It looks very effective planted in borders, rockeries, as edging, or between conifers and heathers.

Luzula maxima (syn. *L. sylvatica*), in its various forms, such as 'Marginata', is particularly good for awkward positions where it is difficult to get other grasses to grow. It is known as the great woodrush and spreads quickly in dry shady places, making it ideal for steep banks, wild garden or woodland. It grows about 30 cm (1 ft) high and spreads 90 cm (3 ft) or more. It is generally considered too invasive to be used amongst border plants or shrubs.

Glyceria spectabile (syn. *G. aquatica*) 'Variegata' is another good ground cover grass where the soil does not dry out. It grows about 2 m (6½ ft) high and 90 cm (3 ft) or more in spread and its green and ivory striped leaves are very effective.

Fig. 12 *Asplenium scolopendrium* (hart's tongue). An evergreen fern which grows well in chalk soils. Height and spread of the broad rich green fronds are about 30 cm (1 ft).

Hardy ferns

Athyrium filix-femina, the lady fern, is a native of Great Britain and forms beautifully lacy green fronds. The male fern, *Dryopteris felix-mas*, has large green fronds. Both grow about 60 cm (2 ft) by 60 cm (2 ft) and like a rich moist soil in slight shade, under trees or shrubs. Unfortunately they are deciduous but their golden brown leaves in autumn are attractive. Another attractive but deciduous fern is *Onoclea sensibilis*, which has light green broad leaves, spreads by underground stems, grows to the same height and likes a similar position to the previous ferns.

Of the evergreen ferns, *Blechnum penna marina* has dark green broad leaves and prefers lime-free moist soils in shade. Height and spread are between 15 and 45 cm (6 and 18 in) by about 30 cm (1 ft). *Asplenium* (syn. *Phyllitis*) *scolopendrium*, hart's tongue (Fig. 12), on the other hand does well on chalk soils and makes good cover planted closely together. The height and spread of its broad rich green fronds are about 30 cm (1 ft).

Polystichum aculeatum and *P. setiferum* are two other versatile evergreens which make good ground cover 90 cm (3 ft) by 90 cm (3 ft) on well-drained soils in a light shady position. Both have very attractive lacy leaves and are an asset to any border. A third elegant fern in this group is *P. polyblepharum* (syn. *braunii*) which also retains its evergreen fronds all year, the mature ones having black stalks. It grows about 45 cm (1½ ft) high and wide.

INDEX